LOUIS KOMZSIK

Wheels in the sky

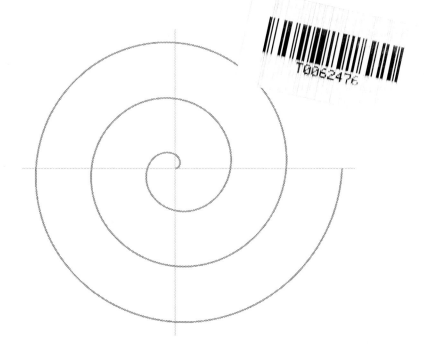

Keep on turning

Trafford Publishing

Readers' comments

"Numerous books have been written popularizing various scientific areas. Fewer have appeared in the area of technology and even less in the combination of both. This book is a bridge between the two areas portraying brilliant and courageous pioneers who advanced the science and technology of the rotational motion throughout the history."

"It is a fascinating look at a common physical phenomenon, rotation. But the discussion is anything but common as the reader is taken on a journey with historical, scientific, mathematical, engineering and sometimes philosophical components woven together. If you are fascinated by how and why questions, this book is a must read. You will discover the genius of some simple observations that gave way to early machines and tools that we all take for granted in our modern society. You will also periodically be looking into the heavens where the same rotational effects are on display in a huge open theater or probing the discovery and effects of rotation on our home planet earth."

Order this book online at www.trafford.com
or email orders@trafford.com

Most Trafford titles are also available at major online book retailers.

Printed in Victoria, BC, Canada.

ISBN: 978-1-4269-3174-1 (soft)
ISBN: 978-1-4269-3175-8 (hard)
ISBN: 978-1-4269-3184-0 (ebook)

*Our mission is to efficiently provide the world's finest, most comprehensive book publishing
service, enabling every author to experience success. To find out how to publish your
book, your way, and have it available worldwide, visit us online at www.trafford.com*

Trafford rev. 4/12/2010

www.trafford.com

North America & international
toll-free: 1 888 232 4444 (USA & Canada)
phone: 250 383 6864 ♦ fax: 812 355 4082

Wheels in the sky

Keep on turning

To those who feel it

Contents

Acknowledgments

I am grateful to my friend, Olivier Schreiber, for his careful and meticulous review, finding many of my mistakes. My former colleague, Gene Poole deserves credit for his valuable recommendations improving the clarity of exposition.

I am indebted to Lily Barabas for representing the physics teacher's perspective and for several corrections. My thanks are also due to Michelle Freret for her diligent review and for validating the interest of the young audience.

I appreciate the contributions of Teresa Nicodemes, Jillian Steele and Leya Taylor at Trafford Publishing, with special thanks to Rian Anderson for the cover art.

Attila Jeney, my high school classmate a long time ago, deserves credit for the quality figures. The photos of planetary phenomena are from public domain sites of NASA. Finally, I also acknowledge Journey and their Infinity, for inspiring the title.

Vernal equinox, 2010
Louis Komzsik

Prologue

Rotation as a motion phenomenon is instrumental in our physical universe. As such, it is mostly unnoticed or unrecognized, and its effects are taken for granted or not understood at all. The goal of this book is to explain, acknowledge and appreciate the powerful and extremely important effects of rotation in our everyday lives.

The invention and subsequent evolution of the mechanical wheel radically elevated humankind's ability to get around and carry objects. The recognition of the round nature of Earth, its rotational motion around the Sun giving us the years, and the rotation of the Earth around its own axis giving us the days of our lives were the next notable rotational effects.

Physically felt effects of rotation are no less intriguing. The everyday phenomenon of a carousel or roller coaster ride, making us scream with joy or becoming sick, are manifestations of rotation on a small scale easily detected by our bodies. Classical physics rules are "bent" in a rotating system that results in the motion of hurricanes and trade winds. Rotation also gives rise to strange phenomena like weighing more or less depending on the direction of our movement relative to the Earth's.

The practical importance of rotation in the very useful rotary machines, providing many conveniences to our lives, is undeniable. Rotational phenomenon still produces new important contributions to human travel. Our ability to find one of the most precious natural resources, oil, using a conceptually simple equipment is priceless. The comfort, stability and control utilized by us every day are important products of rotary machinery.

The planetary levels of rotation were and still are hard to absorb, we are unable to feel wind in our face due to the rotation of the Earth, the most serious argument against it a couple of millenea ago. We certainly cannot feel the rotation of the solar system either, let alone that of the Milky Way, although its spiral shape strongly suggests an influence of a rotational phenomenon. Nevertheless, we can prove those rotations either by observation or actual measurements.

The discussion in the following chapters is mostly descriptive in nature, however, writing a couple of equations at certain points can not be avoided. The depth of these equations does not exceed the common high school level, but the reader troubled by them could skip those over and still enjoy the conceptual aspects of the topic, the rotations in our lives.

1

Turning around

A man was whittling away at a thick branch of a tree cutting off the thin shoots to start a fire and also scraping off the dry, loose bark for the same purpose. The hillside campsite was strategically selected to offer a good view of the animals grazing on the flats and to spot dangerous rival tribes advancing. The evening was peaceful, the members of the tribe were waiting for the fire, the fresh kill of an already skinned animal laying on the ground.

The man finished cleaning the branch and tossed it to the ground nearby. The branch, almost as if it was possessed by spirits, bounced once and started rolling down the hillside. The motion was surprising in its orderliness; the spinning branch was moving downhill at an increasingly faster pace until it came to rest on the flat part of the foothill. The leader and the tribe watched it in amazement, but the sight was soon forgotten because of the cracking of the fire and the heavenly smell of the food.

After all the meat was consumed, even the bones licked dry and chewed on, the leader walked down the hill and brought the branch up again. All anticipated that he was going to drop it into the fire to lengthen the duration of its warmth through the chill of the

night, however, he did not do that. He stepped onto
the edge of the clearing and dropped the branch in the
same spot it was tossed to earlier. The rolling motion
repeated again until the branch stopped in the neighborhood of its earlier rest.

The whole tribe was watching it with an increased interest, as it appeared that the event was now the work
of man and not spirits. The game was then repeated
by other members with similar outcome and the particular branch was saved from its fiery end that night.
Tomorrow will be another day to see if the magic still
worked.

It could have happened this way, although we will
never know.

One thing is for sure, about six thousand years ago
the Egyptians moved very large blocks of stones on
rollers looking like the cleaned branch of our ancient
man on the hillside. It is accepted as the method of
carrying large blocks of stone to great distances at
other ancient monument building sites, such as Stone-
henge. We do not know this for a fact, hoverer, it is
the most plausible by our present day knowledge of
physics.

It is undeniable that recognition of the very first rotational phenomenon by our ancestors resulted in a
tremendous acceleration of the evolution of man. Almost like evolution by revolution, the latter referring
to the rotational effect, the subject of our interest, not
the societal turmoil accompanying the other kind.

Considering the pace of approximately 2 million years of hominid history and about 200,000 years of homo sapiens' presence on the Earth, the last ten thousand years or so are spectacularly accelerated indeed. One cannot but wonder about the important contribution of the rotational phenomenon to this accelerated evolution.

The rotational phenomenon has been utilized much earlier, albeit unrecognized as such. The well known ancient method of starting a fire, spinning a dry stick of wood between the palms with its tip drilling into another flat piece of dry wood, has survived the millenea. Some Amazonian native tribes, still disconnected from the mainstream of the human race and not exposed to modern tools, continue to rely on this method. It was probably the first manifestation of the influence of rotation in our life, while of course friction also played a role in generating the heat to spark the fire.

It was only about six thousand years ago that the actual wheel form, as we know it today, appeared in Mesopotamia. The Sumerians are credited with the invention, and its use enabled them to develop the first agricultural society. Of course, the first wheels were just round pieces of wood with a hole drilled in the center for the axle. To prevent the wheel from rolling off of the axle, a piece of metal, likely of bronze in those times, was fixed in place; the lynchpin as we know it today.

The wheel concept quickly found its way into other cultures. There is archaeological evidence of wheels in Europe and India about five thousand years ago, and in China about four thousand years ago. Its spreading like wildfire appears to be coincident with the domestication of cattle and horses at about the same time. Surely, the biggest benefit of the wheel came along with the invention of the cart pulled by a beast of burden.

Soon, humankind was wheeling around in cattle or horse drawn carriages all over the world, or even using it for entertainment as the Roman chariot races attested. The latter vehicles had more advanced wheels already; the invention of spokes allowed the wheels to be lighter but at the same time stronger. The spokes replaced the wheel's solid wood interior and its circumference was soon built from or at least reinforced by metal.

It is interesting to notice that the ancient American cultures, the Incas and the Aztecs, were lagging behind in the invention of the wheel. It is in part likely due to their isolation and in the case of the Incas it may have also been related to their mountainous terrain that is not very conducive for wheeled travel. There are some archaeological finds of children's toys with wheel like components, but it is still believed that the practical use of wheel arrived in the Americas only in the 16th century with the Spanish conquistadors, incidentally along with the horse.

The next step in the wheel's evolution was even more instrumental in humankind's advancement. A deeper understanding of the rotational phenomenon led to the recognition of wheel's ability to do work. There are archaeological remnants of water wheels in Mesopotamia

and Nubia where they were used for irrigation purposes. The water was scooped up when the buckets
on the circumference of the wheel were in a lower position and when they were raised above the level of the
axis of the wheel the water poured into a canal leading it to irrigate crops. It is a technology still in use
today at some places on Earth where the rotation of
the wheel is still provided by human or animal power.

Not long after that the reverse application also appeared. While scooping water from the moving flow
of rivers, it was recognized that the flow can move the
wheel on its own. Early Chinese evidence from 2-300
BC shows the usage of water power to grind grains.
The wheel was mounted on an axle protruding from
the side of a building and submerged into the water
flow. On the inner end of the axle was a grinding
stone that pulverized the grains on the top of a stationary stone basin.

The Romans developed this art into a science during
the 1st century BC and AD. A historical anecdote is
oft mentioned about the Romans abilities in the use of
water wheels. According to the story, when the Visigoths surrounded Rome in the 6th century AD, they
shut off the aqueducts supplying water to the city.
The Romans suspended water wheels on two boats
and anchored them between the pillars of the river
Tiber where the flow was narrowed down and hence
accelerated. The water lifted out by the water wheels
supplied the city during the siege and the technique
was proven so successful that it was adopted by other
cities in medieval Europe.

The most notable water wheels were installed on the river Thames between the arches of the London Bridge. The plans called for the capability to pump more than one hundred thousand gallons of water per hour to a height of 120 feet, a spectacular engineering feat for those times. The city fathers were, at first, hesitant to allow the construction, but the contractor demonstrated the power of the concept by shooting a water jet over the spire of a nearby church.

The contract was ultimately granted and the wheels were built in the second half of the 16th century. The distribution of the water was by the already existing water pipes, supplying the city for several hundred years from other sources. The wheels were destroyed in the great fire of London in 1666, but were later rebuilt and operated well into the 19th century. A truly spectacular longevity of a Roman invention making virtue out of necessity.

The influence of the first practical application of the rotating phenomenon did not stop there. It appears that once humans recognized the motion and its value, they were actively inventing more and more applications. The ancient engineers were thinking alike their modern successors. Fitting to human nature, the rotational phenomenon soon found its way into warfare. It was already in use in the form of the wheel in war chariots and carrying supplies for the troops, however, a radical step was made in the Greek city of Syracuse by the first mechanical engineer, Archimedes during the third century BC.

Archimedes was born in 287 BC and died defending his hometown in 212 BC. His personal life's details are not well known since his biography was lost, but his mathematical, physical and engineering accomplishments luckily survived the ages. His work in computing the volumes of spheres and cylinders, as well as his rule of objects floating in fluid are well known. It is his engineering work, however, where his understanding and use of the rotational phenomenon yielded the most spectacular results.

He used the concept of the lever and built catapult equipments that threw stones and incendiary devices on the attacking Roman ships. He also developed a pulley system that enabled him to move large weights manually. The concept is now taught in elementary schools and is well understood that the force required to exert a certain pull is lessened by increasing the number of rope lines.

In the case of the Figure 1.1, the force required to lift the object is one half of the weight of the object. Archimedes also realized that there is a price to pay for this advantage in the length of the pull. With the system shown on the figure the person needs to move the end of the rope by twice the distance of the object's motion. This is an early recognition of the conservation of the energy principle.

According to anecdotal evidence, Archimedes actually pulled a captured Roman ship onto the shore with his machinery single-handedly. His statement of "give me a place to stand and I will move the Earth" is part of recorded history and certainly testifies to his confidence in his physics.

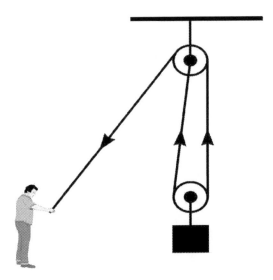

FIGURE 1.1 Archimedes' pulley

Archimedes was one of the first scientists to investigate the properties of mathematical curves, called spirals, such as shown in the cover art. In fact, one of the spirals is called Archimedean spiral in modern mathematics. His spiral is described by a point moving away from its center with a constant radial velocity and simultaneously turning with a constant angular velocity. The latter topics will have immense importance in some of our planetary motions in later chapters.

He also recognized the connection between the spiral shape and physical rotation, which led him to focus his attention to develop a water lifting device more advanced than the ancient water wheel. He placed a screw, just like the ones we use today but with a somewhat deeper thread, into a pipe with a tight fit that still enabled the screw to rotate. When the pipe was submerged into water and the screw turned, it carried the water up toward the top end. The water pouring out at the top was usually captured in another pipe and carried to the place of use, irrigated fields or bath houses.

That the Greeks had baths in his time was a fact commemorated by the anecdote of Archimedes' discovery of the facts of buoyancy. According to the story, upon discovering the rule, he jumped out of his bath and ran down naked on the main street of Syracuse yelling "Eureka" or "I found it".

The screw mechanism itself is really genial as it does not need precision in manufacturing. The surface of the screw is a simple helix, that is generated by wrapping the spiral around a cylinder. If the fit between the screw and the pipe is not tight enough, the water slipping back along the wall just ends up in the turn below and gradually makes its way up.

In a modified version of the design this issue does not even occur, the screw can be affixed solidly to the pipe wall and rotated together. The space between the pipe and the screw surface would gradually carry the water up.

This adaptation of Archimedes' screw was also used

in its reverse form: water was poured in at the top making the pipe and the screw rotate. This rotation may have been connected with a tool and, there it was, the first incarnation of a generator, albeit a mechanical one.

Archimedes' understanding of the rotational phenomenon was far ahead of his time. He was also one of the early converts to the globular Earth concept, a topic of some controversy in ancient times.

2

Being round

Ancient Greek scientists like Archimedes, living on islands surrounded by the Mediterranean Sea or in coastal towns of the mainland, were very familiar with the phenomenon of ships disappearing beyond the horizon in a gradual manner. First the hull disappeared but the sails were visible for a while, then those dipped below the horizon as well. In the converse, the sails and upper structure of ships appeared first when approaching a port, finally followed by the hull.

They also observed the rising or setting of the Sun from or into the sea, depending on their location and orientation. All these observations indicated a round Earth to those who attempted to interpret these phenomena. The round nature of Earth still took a long time to be generally accepted, and there are still some people in denial of that fact.

Credit for a scientific explanation is due to Eratosthenes of Alexandria in the third century BC. He was, as scientists of his time commonly were, a polyhistor: an expert in multiple sciences. He was well versed in astronomy, mathematics, geography and even philosophy. He was the director of the library in Alexandria, by all accounts home of the greatest collection of written material at the time.

According to anecdotal evidence, he heard about the fact that in the southern city of Syene, a vertical stick placed into the ground had no shadow on the day of June 21 at noon. The day was the summer solstice, well known to astronomers of his time. The city of Syene is the modern day Assuan that lies on the Tropic of Cancer, hence the Sun was directly overhead on that day. He discovered, however, that on the same day sticks do cast a shadow in his town, Alexandria. The only explanation he found was that the Earth must be round.

Eratosthenes even thought of an idea for an experiment, shown on Figure 2.1, to measure the circumference of the round Earth. As the story goes, he hired a person to walk and measure the distance from Alexandria to Syene. The measurement yielded about 800 kilometers, in today's units. He measured the shadow of the stick in Alexandria and from it concluded that the angle α on the figure was roughly seven degrees, or about one fiftieth of the 360 degrees comprising a full circle.

Since angles α and β are the same by the teaching of elementary geometry, the two triangles with a curved side are similar. Therefore that ratio of the length of the shadow at Alexandria to the distance to Syene is the same as the ratio of the stick's known height to the radius of the Earth. From this he calculated the radius of the Earth to be about 6,400 kilometers (in today's units) and the total circumference of the Earth as about 50 times the distance from Alexandria to Syene, yielding about 40,000 kilometers. That is

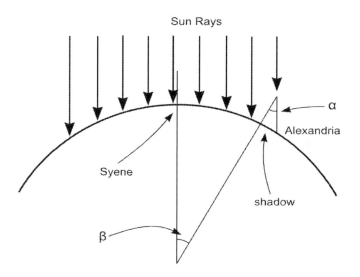

FIGURE 2.1 Eratosthenes' experiment

very close to the 26,000 miles we know today, which is an astonishing accomplishment of the human mind 2,300 years ago.

His results were soon widely known throughout the Mediterranean and by the beginning of our times the Earth was almost always depicted as a globe. This discovery enabled an entirely new interpretation of celestial observations and suddenly things were looked at in a different framework.

Incidentally, the wide acceptance and visible proof of

the Earth's roundness did not satisfy a group of people. They, commonly called the flat-Earthers, remained in objection unbelievably all the way to this millenea. The circular shadow of the Earth on the Moon would not convince them. They would invent a circular disk description of the Earth. That would certainly explain the circular shadow, assuming that the Sun dips below the plane of the disk at night.

Their description of the arrangement of the known facts about the Earth's surface was so inventive that it is worthy of a brief discussion. In its most advanced form, their belief was that the North Pole was at the center of the Earth disk and the continents were arranged in their known relations, but the perimeter of the Earth was the icy mountains of the South Pole.

One needs some imagination to follow this, but let us indulge as an exercise. The circumnavigation of the Earth by Magellan in 1522, just three decades after Columbus' voyage to America, was explained by the flat Earth believers in their characteristically inventive way. In their vision it was akin to sailing around an island. They posited that the circumnavigation was only possible in East-West directions and not North-South, because then the ship would fall off at the edge of the Earth, assuming it was able to cross the icy waters and iceberg barriers. In fact the icebergs were there for the particular purpose of defending the foolish who attempted to do just that.

The strength of delusion of the flat-Earthers was still highly present in 19th century England leading to one of the most famous scientific bets ever. The bet involved Alfred Russel Wallace, a self-taught British naturalist of humble origins. Wallace was born into a poor family and had only a grade school education. He spent his teenage years doing various jobs but due to science museum visits during his school years he never gave up on his dream of becoming a scientist.

Eventually he got an opportunity to be a specimen collector in the East Indies working for a botanical company. During his stay on the island of Ternate, at the time a Dutch territory, he came upon an explanation of how species evolved. He called his theory the theory of transmutation and wrote a letter explaining it to Charles Darwin, the best known naturalist in England at the time. He asked Darwin to present it to the academic society. What came next was a bit murky and there are several interpretations of it.

Darwin apparently was working on the same idea at the time, but was delaying its publication. His academic friends withheld Wallace's paper for a year until Darwin completed his own manuscript and rushed to print it. By some accounts Wallace's letter gave Darwin the missing idea he was searching for to explain his own observations. By other accounts Darwin just needed the jolt to complete his own work in order to claim priority, because he still had some unanswered questions.

Wallace, a good sport, conceded credit to Darwin, but many people now acknowledge Wallace as the co-discoverer of the evolution. Intriguingly Darwin, who went on to fame and fortune, provided financial help to Wallace later in his life, who struggled to make a living. Whether it was guilt or just friendly help, we will never know. However, Wallace's good nature also led him to his involvement with the flat Earth bet.

A Christian philosopher named John Hampden, one of the arch proponents of the flat Earth principle, originated the bet. The mainstream flat Earth believers were strongly motivated by religious beliefs and ardently adhered to the Bible. Hampden, however, having been educated at Oxford, decided to use science to prove his biblical beliefs. In January of 1870 he proposed a 500 pound bet in the Scientific Opinion, a leading forum at the time. The bet was a challenge to prove the roundness of the Earth by everyday means, understandable by a commoner untrained in the sciences.

Most of the scientific community considered the bet a joke, almost all of the people in the country ignored it, but Wallace took up the challenge. He claimed to do it as a public service to the people and in the interest of society. He may have been drawn to the amount of the prize, considering that by that time he was back in England with a family and without a stable academic job. This was not a surprise, after all he did not have a college degree and people did not yet recognize his contribution to Darwin's theory; they do so only reluctantly even today.

Wallace of course knew the phenomenon all seafarers and coastal people knew, that the surface of the ocean also curves and the ships gradually disappear under the horizon. He devised a land experiment to exploit the same phenomenon.

He chose the Old Bedford Canal, a uniquely straight man-made canal in Bedforshire, specifically a six mile long open section of it with an un-obstructed view between two bridges. Wallace computed that the curvature of the Earth would be visible in a distance of six miles. He placed long poles into the water at every mile with exactly six foot long sections above the waterline at each location. The poles were also marked at every foot in height. He expected that the curvature would be shown when viewing the markings on the posts with a telescope.

Sure enough, the experiment showed that the middle pole was about 4 feet higher than the first and the last poles at the two bridges, to which the telescope was aligned to present the horizontal "flat" Earth. The second and fourth poles also showed the proper height difference. To all rational minds and to the judge present the proof was adequate. Wallace proved the roundness of the Earth and the bet amount was released to him by the judge.

What followed was a testimonial to the irrational mind-set of the believers of the flat Earth philosophy. Hampden refused to accept the proof. In fact, he blatantly insisted that it actually proved that the Earth was flat. He continued to fight, even threatened Wallace's family. The latter act sent Hampden to jail, ultimately completely disgraced. He lived the rest of his days in poverty but never gave up his conviction of a flat Earth. Following Hampden's crusade, a flat Earth society of England was founded, later grandiosely renamed to be that of the World.

The philosophy is still with us today. The latest manifestation of the belief was the International Flat Earth Research Society of America, organized and led by a California couple. Ironically they lived in the Palmdale area close to Edwards Air Force base, the landing site of the space shuttle after completing its orbits around the round Earth. They had a regular newsletter with many subscribers as recently as the beginning of this millenea. It was a long lived faulty belief, indeed.

3

Rolling circles

Another enduring fallacy was the view that the Earth was the center of the universe, independently of its flatness or roundness. Many Greek scientists in the first milleneum BC were fully convinced of the central role of Earth. The rotation of all other objects around us was duly noted, except in some cases with foolish sounding explanations.

The Aristotelian system, named after the most famous philosopher of those times, consisted of 56 transparent concentric spheres rotating around the Earth. The Moon was on the innermost sphere and the reason for the large number of spheres was because they were used to justify some of the inexplicable behavior of the planets.

There were several plausible arguments supporting the view. If the Earth was moving, we should see a relative motion of the stars, which one could not. Then there was the rather obvious fact that we could not feel the air moving in our face when the Earth moved. The assumed coup de grace was, however, the fact that the apparent brightness of Venus does not change and Aristotle's followers thought that could not happen otherwise but with Venus circling Earth. Of course the simple explanation of Venus as an inner

planet on a concentric circle with Earth did not occur
to them yet. They also glossed over the fact that the
Earth centered concentric spheres could not account
for the changes in brightness of some of the planets
that moved around in different distance from us.

One of the earliest attempts at explaining the world
with the Sun at the center was made by the Greek
Aristarchos in the third century B.C. He was born on
the island of Samos and is still famous for his attempts
at measuring the distance of the Earth and the Moon.
In his book that survived the ages, titled *On the sizes
and distances of the Sun and Moon*, he presented a
heliocentric view. Aristarchos' measurements were a
bit inaccurate, but considering the tools available for
him at the time his reasoning and approach was sound.

He recognized that the Moon and the Sun have the
same visual angles when viewed from the Earth during an eclipse and conjectured correctly that then their
sizes should be related to their distances. He then calculated that the Sun is about seven times farther away,
hence seven times bigger in diameter than the Moon.
This was somewhat smaller than the now known value
of about 400, but he correctly concluded that it is im-
possible that the much larger Sun would orbit around
the much smaller Earth as fast as once a day. Therefore he arrived at his heliocentric view.

He concluded that the stars are very far away and
that is the reason we do not see any relative motion
between them, as opposed to the observations about
Earth and our celestial partners. He also concluded
that the Sun was just another star, the closest to us.

He was of course on the right track, but his ground-breaking heliocentric thinking was not accepted at the time of his life.

Somewhat in the taste of the religious persecution of scientists in the middle ages to come, he was also accused of violating the prudence of the prevailing philosophically grounded arrangement of the universe. It is unclear whether there was a formal court case against him, but he was publically admonished by several of his contemporaries. Some simply rejected the heliocentric system because Aristarchos was not yet able to explain the peculiar motions of Venus and Mars.

The Earth centered view prevailed for centuries even after his time and was further set back by the work of Ptolemaeus. Claudius Ptolemaeus was born a Roman citizen, but of Greek or, according to some sources, maybe Egyptian ethnicity. He is now known by the English version of his name, Ptolemy, and he personally delayed humankind's understanding of our surroundings for about a milleneum. Despite Aristarchos' hypothesis, that was yet unproven at the time, Ptolemy convinced the world otherwise.

Ptolemy in the second century AD "proved" that the center of the universe was the Earth by explaining that the Sun, the other planets and the stars were rotating around us on concentric spheres. The spheres were actually made of crystal, as he said, something was needed to hold them up there in lieu of knowledge about gravity. Ptolemy's book titled *Almagest* became widely known and due to his academic reputation was accepted at face value for centuries.

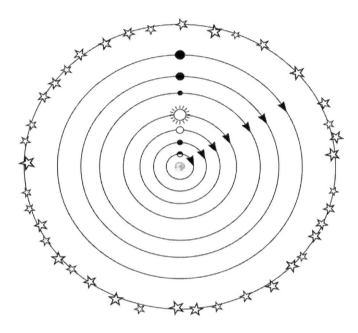

FIGURE 3.1 The Ptolemy model

In his view the order of the then known celestial objects from the central Earth outward was Moon, Mercury, Venus, Sun, Mars, Jupiter and Saturn, as shown on Figure 3.1. They were all rotating in the same direction. It is notable that even though the Earth was supposed to be fixed in his system, the rest of the solar system was rotating. This is a testament to the early recognition of the intrinsic nature of the rotational motion, the premise of our book.

Ptolemy of course noticed that those circular paths of the celestial objects were far from perfect. Some of them appeared to speed up or slow down, and even go backwards in certain segments. This was a serious problem of the model and the so-called retrograde motion of Mars was a thorn in his side. Finally, he invented an explanation to this by introducing another set of crystal balls (pun intended).

His idea was based on the Greek mathematicians' penchant for the circle and the wealth of intriguing curves generated by rolling circles. Rolling circles on a plane and observing the motion of certain points resulted in peculiar patterns, called cycloids. Depending on the ratio of the horizontal motion of the circle and the angular velocity of the rolling circle, an observed point located on the circle generated various curves.

The curves were smoothly waving when the speed of the linear motion of the circle was large in comparison to the angular speed. When their ratio was at a specific value equating the linear distance covered during one full revolution with the circumference, the curves created a sharp cusp. Finally, when the rotation was faster than the linear motion, the curves produced pronounced loops.

The latter shape gave an idea to Ptolemy for an engineous explanation of the observed phenomenon. He explained that Mars is actually on a smaller crystal ball that is rolling inside of the big ball of the sky. This motion, shown on Figure 3.2 is somewhat plausible. The partial circle with the large radius represents the circle along which the center of the smaller crystal ball moves. The full circle represents the smaller crystal ball. Following the point of Mars on the circumference of that circle will result in a looping motion of the cycloid curve.

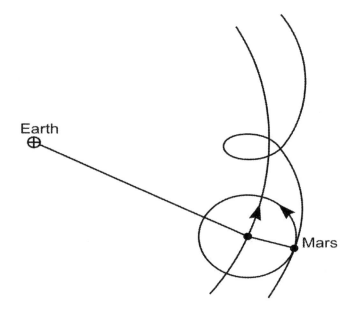

FIGURE 3.2 Mars cycles

Apart from the incorrectness of this explanation, Ptolemy was an accomplished astronomer. He would observe the stars, would make notes of their locations, apparent brightness and would even predict certain eclipses. His belief that the Earth was the center of the organized motions he observed in the sky was not unnatural and quite common in his time. It was certainly in accordance with the observations about the stability and unchanging nature of the Earth as opposed to the nightly or monthly changing heavenly phenomena.

His remaining problem was that the timing was not in compliance with practical observations. Ptolemy was never able to explain the discrepancies, nevertheless, for almost 1,500 years after his time his wrong celestial vision prevailed. Ptolemy was, however, not the only person to be faulted for this. Some of the blame is to be placed on the Catholic Church of the middle ages.

The Earth centric vision was perfectly fitting with the biblical references to Creation and the church defended it to the bitter end. The acceptance of a moving Earth would relegate it to be just another one of the lowly planets, like Mars or Venus. This would remove it from being the center point of God's creation.

This was certainly not appealing to the Catholic church and they were staunch defenders of Ptolemy's vision until the 1500's. The second half of the 16th century became a bloody conflict over this topic, culminating in the death of Giordano Bruno at the burning stake in 1600.

Giordano Bruno was an ordained priest, hence his beliefs were considered even more blasphemous by the church. Besides his heliocentric views, he also confessed to believing in the infiniteness of the universe and the possibility of other worlds.

This was another unacceptable view to the church at the time. The scientific truth, however, could not be held back, and incidentally another member of the clergy brought the final resolution in the topic of revolution.

4

Rotating world

Nicolaus Copernicus was born in 1473 in the northern part of Poland. He put the issue of the center of the world finally to rest, although his explanation took another hundred years or so to gain full acceptance. He studied at the Cracow Collegium in the 1490s and spent the first years of the 1500s in Italy studying science and medicine. Upon returning to Poland, his uncle, the bishop of Frauenburg in the northernmost diocese of the Catholic church, took him under his wing. He appointed his nephew a canon of the diocese in 1511, a role Copernicus fulfilled until his death in 1543.

The three decades in the position allowed him to immerse into deep thinking and research about the motion of celestial objects, specifically into the discrepancies between Mars' orbit and the Ptolemy model. Copernicus discovered that by simply switching our central role with the Sun, suddenly more facts were falling into place. The observed motion of the planets would fit the model and there was no need for concocted adjustments.

It is an interesting footnote of history that the quiet cleric's work could have been lost, had it not been for the acute interest of a young German professor from the University of Wittenberg, Georg Joachim Rheticus. During the late 1530s Rheticus heard rumors about the groundbreaking work of the Polish canon and in 1539 he traveled to visit him for a few weeks. Copernicus, who never had a student as he has not been affiliated with any university, welcomed the young scientist and Rheticus' weeks of visit turned into two years.

During those years Rheticus fully understood and appreciated the work, and he was able to convince Copernicus to publish it. Rheticus took the manuscript with him to Nürnberg in 1541 and arranged for printing. With the technology of the time this was extremely time consuming and took the better part of 1542. Finally, he returned to Copernicus in 1543, who was on his deathbed by that time, just waiting to see his life's work published before his death. The publication year of the book *De Revolutionibus Orbium Coelestium*, loosely translated into English as "the revolutions of celestial orbits", hence shares the year of his death.

Copernicus' world view is shown on Figure 4.1. The order of the world now is Sun, Mercury, Venus, Earth (with Moon rotating around it), followed by the outer planets Mars, Jupiter and Saturn. The remaining planets were still not known. It is notable that the fixed stars were not anymore affixed to the outermost circle in his vision, but randomly distributed within the universe.

The view's credibility was significantly boosted by the fact that it simply explained the evening appearances of Venus. This was of course the result of Venus

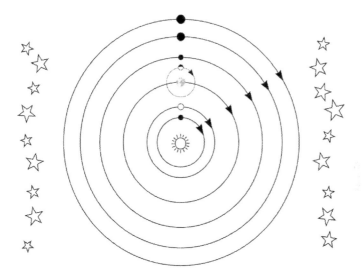

FIGURE 4.1 The Copernican model

being an inner planet closer to the Sun than Earth. The view also immediately resolved Mars' retrograde motion issue as shown on Figure 4.2, that required the epicyclic device of Ptolemy.

In the figure it is clearly visible that the different relative positions of Mars and Earth produce the apparent retrograde motion. Since the Earth is closer to the Sun than Mars, counter-intuitive things happen. When the Earth is in position 1, the line of sight to Mars would show the position of Mars in point 1 in the sky.

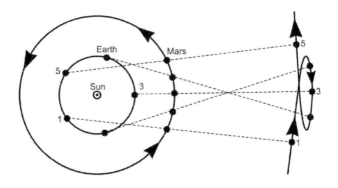

FIGURE 4.2 Mars retrograde motion

When moving through point 3, Mars is bypassed by Earth moving on an inner circle giving the appearance of Mars moving backwards against the sky. When reaching point 5, Mars has again resumed its forward motion, until another cycle is completed.

It is ironic, however, that Mars' retrograde motion was not completely resolved by the Copernican model either. Whereas Ptolemy's now obviously incorrect model placed the Mars ahead of its observed position, Copernicus' model made it delay somewhat. The acceptance of Copernicus' model now hinged on this final discrepancy.

Galileo Galilei played a leading role in the struggle to gain acceptance of the Copernican model. Galileo was born in 1564 and is often called the "father of modern astronomy". He was born, brought up and educated in Pisa, except for a few teenage years in Florence when his family lived there. He undertook medical studies at the university in Pisa obeying his father's request, but studied mathematics for his own interest. Ultimately he even received a professorship of mathematics at the university. After only three years he moved to the university of Padua for two decades of fruitful work during which he made many of his now famous observations.

Galileo, who became the leading astronomer at the time and probably the most influential of all times, started exploring the sky with a telescope. According to anecdotal evidence, he only heard about the concept of the telescope and based on that he built his own. His telescope produced a twenty fold magnification and opened up his celestial horizon to include objects that had not been seen until then. His telescope would also allow him to narrow the aperture and observe very bright objects with more definition. Galileo may have been the first person to say: "Seeing is believing".

This led him to observations of Jupiter during the early part of 1610 and soon he discovered that there were four moons rotating around Jupiter. He named the moons after the Medicis, the noble family sponsoring his scientific pursuits. His observations also proved that our Moon does rotate around the Earth, even if the Earth is rotating around the Sun. Galileo published his findings in 1610 in a book titled *Sidereus nuncius*, translated as Starry Messenger, and he became an overnight scientific sensation, even with the limited speed of information travel of his time.

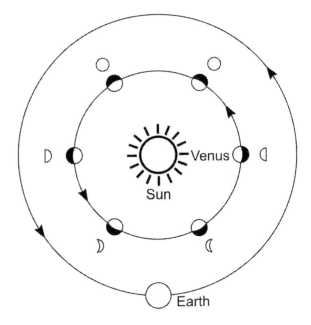

FIGURE 4.3 The phases of Venus

He continued his celestial observations for the next two decades. He also observed the phases of Venus, shown on Figure 4.3, to be in agreement with a Sun centric arrangement. Galileo explained that if Venus were on a circular orbit around Earth the sequence of the phases of the Venus could never match the observations. Since Venus could have not been rotating around the Earth, hence the phases of Venus contradicted the Ptolemaic vision.

He considered this fact to be the final proof of the Copernican view. He published his thinking in 1632 in a book titled *Dialogue concerning the two chief world systems* and that finally drew the full wrath of the Catholic church on him. He was also charged with heresy like Giordano Bruno, but due to his personal connection to the Pope his life was spared. The Pope would commute Galileo's sentence on the condition that he recanted his views and confined him to house arrest for the last decade of his life.

The reason that the idea of the Earth rotating around the Sun took so long to be accepted was, however, not only due to the religious objection. Intuition was against it. People thought that when someone dropped a weight from a tower on the west side, it should fall farther away from the wall, due to the rotation of the Earth. Conversely, the weight dropped on the eastern side would have to hit the wall. Since neither of these happened in experiments, the belief was held that the Earth does not move.

Galileo died in 1642 and by the end of the 17th century the moving Earth belief was widely held. The Vatican, however, took another 300 years to make an official statement about the church's mistakes regarding Bruno and Galileo. It took the arrival of the non-

Italian Pope, John-Paul II to acknowledge "the error
of the theologians of the time". In his statement he
singled out the treatment of Galileo as one of the mistakes committed by the zeal of the inquisitors.

The still remaining discrepancy of Mars' motion, its
apparent delay from the model was not due to Copernicus' Sun-centric model. It was due to the fact that
the orbits in question were not circles, a fact only recognized about a century later.

5

Elliptic cycles

Johannes Kepler was born in 1571 in Germany and was educated in the protestant school system of the town of Maulbronn. He later studied at the university of Tübingen with the goal of becoming a priest. He was, however, more interested in astronomy and was introduced to the then radical ideas of Copernicus. Before ordainment, he took on a job opportunity as a high school mathematics teacher in Graz, Austria, hence he is sometimes referred to as Austrian.

His double interest in astronomy and mathematics made him recognize the coincidence that there were five other planets besides Earth and there were also five regular polyhedra. The five extraterrestrial planets known at his time were Mercury, Venus, Mars, Jupiter and Saturn. The regular polyhedra have regular polygon sides, like the hexahedron or the common cube with square sides. Others are the tetrahedron, the octahedron and the icosahedron with four, eight and twenty equilateral triangle sides, respectively. The fifth one is the dodecahedron with twelve pentagonal faces. Kepler imagined an intrinsic connection between the two facts and created a vision of the universe where the known planets were all nested in one of the regular solids.

We now know of course that this was incorrect, however, his work raised enough attention in the scientific circles that in 1599 he was invited by the famous Danish astronomer Tycho Brahe to Prague where the latter was the court astronomer of German Emperor Rudolf. Brahe had amassed a wealth of celestial observations during his illustrious career, but he was somewhat of a rowdy personality. He was involved in a duel and almost died of a sword inflicted wound. He also had his own hypothesis about the order in our solar system.

This otherwise head-strong and aggressive person in this particular case settled to making a compromise between Ptolemy and Copernicus. Or maybe he was astutely judging the society and erred on the side of political correctness. Brahe retained the Earth as the center of universe and kept the Sun orbiting around it, thereby appeasing the religious authorities. Quite smartly, however, he placed the other planets onto an orbit around the Sun. This allowed a better agreement with his precise observations without making the clergy irate.

Brahe was rather disorganized and he invited Kepler to assist him in organizing his observations. Two years after Kepler's arrival, however, in 1601 Brahe suddenly died of an over-indulgence in eating and drinking (another apparently age old trait of humankind) and Kepler was named royal astronomer. He inherited Brahe's life time observation collection and that was the basis of his work about Mars.

Brahe's celestial model did not solve the Mars problem of Copernicus' model either, just as Copernicus did not fully solve Ptolemy's Mars problem, but his observations provided Kepler the data to prevail. He worked on this topic for the better part of a decade before he realized that the common assumption made by all three of the universal models was wrong. They all assumed that the planets move in circles with constant speeds and with either the Earth (in Ptolemy's vision) or the Sun (in Copernicus and Brahe's visions) in the center of the motion. They were all wrong!

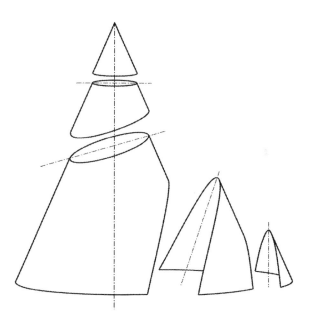

FIGURE 5.1 Conic sections

Kepler realized that planets move along ellipses, not

circles, with the Sun as one of the focal points of the ellipse. Ellipses as geometric objects were well known by the ancient Greek geometers as a member of the class of curves called conic sections. These curves are obtained by cutting a circular cone (like an ice cream cone) by a plane in various directions.

Cutting a circular cone perpendicularly to the axis produces the circle, while cutting it somewhat slanted results in the elongated circular shape of the ellipse. The cuts more inclined will result in two more shapes that will have some planetary importance in our discussions later, the parabola and the hyperbola. Figure 5.1 demonstrates those cuts and the resulting curves.

Kepler's ellipses were still in line with the Copernican view of the planets rotating around the Sun, after all circles were just special cases of ellipses. It also helped that the ellipses in question were very much circle like, at least in the case of the inner planets. This was an extremely important distinction, however, especially so in connection with Mars.

Mars' orbit that caused so much grief for a milleneum, troubling both Ptolemy and Copernicus, had a ratio of the two axes as 0.9956. This is very close to one so it is almost a circle, but just elliptic enough to make the earlier models inaccurate. Finally, the issue of Mars' motion was correctly explained in his book titled *De Stella Martis.*

The remaining issue bothering Kepler was the apparently uneven cycles of various planets during the duration of one turn. He asked: Why would they accelerate and decelerate?

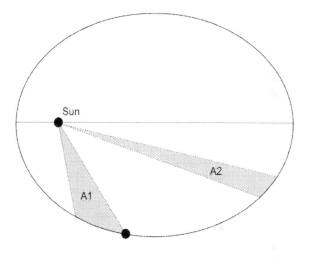

FIGURE 5.2 Kepler's laws

Kepler concluded based on his calculations that the areal velocity of the planets is constant in rotation. That means that the sections denoted by A1 and A2 on Figure 5.2 have equal area. When the planet, depicted by the dot on the circumference of the ellipse, was in close proximity to the focus the Sun occupied, it was moving faster and covered a wider swath of the orbit. Due to the proximity, however, the lines between the Sun and the planet position were shorter.

On the other hand, when the planet was on the opposite side from the Sun, the lengths of the lines were much longer, hence the angle of the section narrower. The two areas, however, were the same. Therefore the orbital speed of the planet was smaller on the far side. This recognition was quite extraordinary, based on pure observations, attesting to Kepler's genius. This became Kepler's second law.

Kepler also explained how several planets could occupy distinct elliptical orbits around the same Sun. He realized that they are located in a slightly different orbital plane of the solar system, hence they can peacefully coexist in the glare of the common Sun.

Kepler published his new world order in a book titled *Astronomia Nova* at the end of the first decade of the 17th century. Not surprisingly the leading scientists of the time did not endorse it. After all, circles were so beautifully symmetric, why would God create some ugly squashed circles? Some even attempted to recreate the elliptic pattern, that was now indisputable from Brahe's observations, with circles and cycloids like Ptolemy. The world had to wait for Newton to prove that Kepler was right.

Kepler also observed that the outer planets, farther away from the Sun orbit on less circle like, elongated ellipses and at higher speeds as well. This observation led him to his third law stating that the square of the orbital period of a planet is proportional to the cube of the mean distance of the planet from the Sun. The mean distance is the average of the distance between the planet's closest (perihelion) position to the Sun and its farthest (aphelion).

According to this law the orbital period of a planet around the Sun is

$$\sqrt{K \cdot D^3}$$

where D is the mean distance and K is the so-called Kepler constant that depends on the mass of the planet. The value of K for Earth is $4.03 \cdot 10^{-29}$. Earth's mean distance from the Sun is about 150,000 kilometers, or $1.5 \cdot 10^{11}$ meters. Using the formula above, the term under the square root becomes $13.3 \cdot 10^4$ days, resulting in our well known orbital period of 365 days.

TABLE 5.1
Orbital periods

Planet	Distance	Period
Mercury	0.387	0.241
Venus	0.723	0.616
Earth	1	1
Mars	1.524	1.88
Jupiter	5.203	11.9
Saturn	9.539	29.5
Uranus	19.191	84.0
Neptune	30.071	165.0
Pluto	39.457	248.0

Table 5.1 shows the mean distance from the Sun and the orbital time computed by Kepler's third law for all the planets now known in our solar system. The numbers are normalized relative to the Earth's motion.

The period is measured in years and the distances are in astronomical units, the mean distance of the Earth. Ellipses of our solar system are truly enormous!

Kepler's law for Mars with $K = 3.95 \cdot 10^{-29}$ and using Mars' mean distance from the Sun as 225,000 kilometers yields an orbital period of 684 days. The next planet in our solar system Jupiter has a Kepler constant of $K = 3.98 \cdot 10^{-29}$ but with over five times bigger mean distance. Jupiter will observe a rather long year with 4,331 days.

The distances and times of the outer planets are mind-boggling. For example, for Neptune Table 5.1 indicates a mean distance of about 30 times that of the Earth and a 165 Earth years long orbital time. Poor Pluto is even farther out and recently had to suffer the disgrace of being removed from the list of planets by some newly established planetary standards.

The most radical demonstrations of the elongated elliptical orbits are the orbits of comets. This was recognized by an English astronomer, Edmund Halley, about a hundred years after Kepler. He was born in 1656 to a wealthy family enabling him to pursue scientific interests, specifically astronomy. He knew of medieval written records about bright, fast objects occasionally appearing in our solar system at a very steep angle compared to the orbit of the planets and disappearing again forever.

Halley recognized that those records may be talking about one particular object regularly appearing, but with a very long orbit time; a comet. The comet

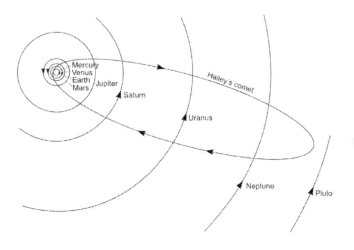

FIGURE 5.3 Halley's comet

took an appearance during Halley's life in 1682 and Halley observed its path carefully. He predicted that the comet would reappear in 1758, when he would be 102. Such prediction was not really taken seriously, until the comet did reappear as Halley predicted. The object has been then named Halley's comet.

The comet whose path is shown on Figure 5.3, takes about 76 years to complete its elongated elliptical orbit. When it is the farthest away from the Sun, in its aphelion position, it is about 5.3 billion kilometers away, almost reaching Pluto's orbit. In its perihelion position it is inside even Venus' orbit only about 90 million kilometers from the Sun. This is an extremely long axis of an elliptical orbit, essentially the radius of the solar system, especially now that Pluto has been pulled from the ranks of planets.

Even Kepler's genius in observations and their mathematical explanations did not extend to the understanding of the cause of the motions. He held some vague belief about a "magnetic" connection between them. The understanding ultimately came from Halley's friend, Isaac Newton.

6

Twirling planets

The fundamental phenomenon of gravity was first recognized and explained by Newton. In the early ages of humanity the reluctance of accepting the sphericity of Earth in part was fueled by the lack of awareness to gravity. Not knowing the effect of gravity, it was a rational argument that people on the southern hemisphere would fall off a round Earth.

Isaac Newton, arguably the most influential scientist of all times, was born on a farm in Lincolnshire, England in the last days of 1642. Incidentally that was the same year Galileo Galilei died. It seems like a historical baton was being passed between two giants of science. Newton was raised by his grandmother until his teenage years and following his uncle's prodding he went to Cambridge when he turned 18. His prodigy in science and mathematics became apparent during those years. After graduation with a Bachelor's degree he returned home and spent two years in private study and deep thinking.

According to one of his biographers, during that time on a warm evening Newton was having tea in the apple orchard behind the family house. He noticed an apple falling and hitting the ground with a thud. He then realized that a mysterious force was pulling the apple to

the ground, a force extending considerably higher than
the apple tree and likely even reaching the Moon. He
also realized that the force was acting on everything,
including our own bodies.

Newton went back to Cambridge and spent several
decades on establishing the foundation of many scientific areas, most importantly that of the physics of
gravitation and motion. His law of gravitation states
that two bodies, with masses M and m and a distance
R between them, will pull on each other with the force
of

$$G\frac{M \cdot m}{R^2},$$

where G is the universal gravity constant, a difficult
to measure tiny quantity of $6.6 \cdot 10^{-11}$ in the metric
system of measurements where the masses are in kilograms and the distance is in meters. More interesting about this constant is that it is intrinsic to our
universe and applicable between any pair of masses.
Imagining M being the mass of the Earth and m the
mass of the apple, the force describes the falling apple
phenomenon. Interestingly the formula says nothing
about the volume or shape of the objects, an appealing but tough to accept fact.

Newton explained that the mass of an object defines
its inertia, a topic of some intrigue in later chapters. If
an object had twice the mass of another one, it also re-
sisted a motion two times more strongly. This observation led to Newton's second law of motion stating that
the force required to move an object is proportional to
its mass and acceleration, the famous $F = m \cdot a$.

Newton recognized that each object in the solar system has its own gravitational field which influences the other objects in its vicinity. The force of course diminishes by the square of the distance between the objects' center of mass, and the larger the masses are the bigger the force is. But his main and most influential realization was that the planets are being twirled around by the force of gravity!

Newton's universal gravity law applied to a body on the surface of the Earth simplifies, since the distance becomes the earth's radius. Introducing the term of the acceleration of gravity as

$$g = G\frac{M}{R^2},$$

the gravitational pull of the Earth on a body, also known as its weight, becomes the well known formula of $W = m \cdot g$. The form is now in accordance with Newton's second law of motion stated above.

Assuming a person with a mass of 100 kilograms and using Earth's acceleration of gravity value of 9.81 meters per second squared, the person's weight is $m \cdot g = 981$ kilogram meters per second squared, or Newton in the metric system of measurements.

For those preferring the English system of measurements the acceleration of gravity of the Earth is about 32.2 feet per second squared. The weight of the person of 200 pounds in mass would be 6,440 pound feet per second squared and this number is rather unfamiliar. The issue we face here is an ambiguity of the English system: there is a pound mass and there is a pound force, and they are two different units.

What happens is that in the everyday use of the term weight, we really mean mass. When we purchase a pound of flour in the grocery store and the label also says something about 0.45 kilogram, we see that the English unit is meant to be the pound mass. Otherwise their relationship would not be correct. So, when we step on the bathroom scale, despite the fact that it actually measures our weight, it shows our mass. The 200 pound person is about 90 kilograms.

Table 6.1 shows the absolute value of the acceleration of gravity of solar system objects in increasing order, as well as the relative values with respect to the Moon, the smallest planetary object on the list.

TABLE 6.1
Acceleration of gravity

Object	Absolute	Relative
Moon	1.63	1
Mercury	3.7	2.27
Mars	3.73	2.29
Venus	8.87	5.44
Uranus	9.01	5.53
Earth	9.81	6.02
Saturn	11.19	6.87
Neptune	11.28	6.92
Jupiter	25.93	15.91
Sun	274.1	168.2

The table demonstrates the reason why the same

person weighs less on the surface of the Moon than on the Earth. The Moon's acceleration of gravity is about one sixth of the Earth's. The astronauts participating in Moon landings demonstrated this fact with their exuberant skipping and world record breaking jumping on the grainy films we have seen in the past. Whether those were Moon record breaking jumps, is a question we cannot answer yet.

The fact is that our weight is a force, resulting from the acceleration of gravity. The acceleration of gravity is in essence the strength of the gravity field acting on the object. It measures the rate of the increase in the speed of a falling body toward Earth. Newton's famous predecessor, Galileo Galilei, hero of an earlier chapter, in the early 1600's devised a simple experiment at the leaning tower of Pisa.

Galileo demonstrated that a wooden ball with the same shape as an iron ball reaches the ground at the same time, when dropped from the high tower. He concluded that the acceleration of a body in free fall is constant, assuming the shape of the bodies is the same and they do not incur a measurable amount of air resistance. He just could not explain why, and the question confounded scientists for decades until correctly answered by Newton.

Gravity is the main reason for the difficulties making aircraft leave Earth and reach space. For example, it requires tremendous energy to lift a space shuttle off the ground. The velocity required for an object to escape the confines of the gravity field of a planet is, however, independent of the mass of the object. The

bigger the mass the more energy is needed to accelerate the object to the escape velocity, but the required
velocity is the same.

More specifically, the escape velocity is the initial
speed required from a stationary position in the gravitational field. As such it is measured at the surface
of the Earth, assuming we are focusing on an object
escaping our planet. On average, the escape velocity
from the Earth is about 11.2 kilometers per second
or almost 7 miles per second. That velocity is about
ten times the speed of a bullet shot from a good rifle. Clearly, we need an extremely good rifle to shoot
something out of the Earth's gravitational field.

This value of escape velocity assumes that the object is shot up in a radial direction from the Earth
and needs to fight against the gravitational field. The
Earth itself, however, could help us in this endeavor.
Since Earth's angular velocity (due to the spinning
around its axis, the subject of our next chapter) at
the Equator is about 0.465 kilometers per second, if
we launch our object to the east horizontally, we only
need about 10.735 kilometers per second escape velocity. It does not seem much of a difference, but when
considering the energy needs of practical objects (certainly larger than a bullet), this makes a significant
difference. This is the reason launch sites near the
equator are sought, like French Guyana for the European space programs, or as south on the continent as
possible like in the case of Cape Canaveral.

When an object is already in an orbit around the
Earth, it has a smaller escape velocity. Figure 6.1

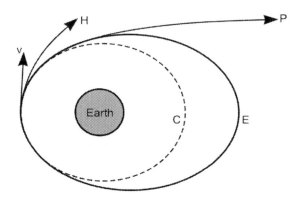

FIGURE 6.1 Escape from the planet Earth

demonstrates potential orbits around Earth. The ellipse denoted by E and the circle C are orbits of an
object with less than the escape velocity. The object will remain in the gravitational hold of the Earth.
One could consider the circular orbit being that of our
Moon. When the object reaches or exceeds the escape
velocity, it will leave the Earth on either a parabolic
(P) or a hyperbolic (H) trajectory, respectively.

There are some natural exhibitors of the escape phenomenon. The haphazardly flying planetary objects,
comets or other rogue elements in the universe all es-

caped from the leash of gravity of some planet at some
stage in their lives.

On the other hand, entering into the gravitational
field of a planet, albeit temporarily, leads to a powerful technique called the gravitational sling shot. This
technique uses the gravitational field of a planet to
increase the velocity of an object. This increase in
velocity is with respect to the Sun, assuming we are
concerned about objects in our solar system. It does
not change the velocity of the object relative to the
planet whose gravitational field is used for the assis-
tance.

Let us imagine the scenario of an interplanetary object approaching a planet with a velocity v while the
planet is moving in the direction of the object with
a velocity of u. Both of these velocities are with respect to the solar system. If the object achieves a
close enough path to the planet to be "captured" by
its gravitational field, then the planet is going to pull
the object. Due to this pull, the object is going to at-
tain a parabolic or hyperbolic orbit around the planet.
Because the velocity of the object is larger than the
escape velocity of the orbit, the object will leave the
planet's field in the opposite direction.

During the approach the relative speed of the object
and the planet was $u + v$ as they were moving toward
each other. Upon leaving the planet's gravitational
hold, the object's relative speed to the planet is still
$u + v$. However, since they are now moving in the
same direction, the object's speed relative to the solar
system is $2 \cdot u + v$. In summary, the object gained an

additional $2 \cdot u$ speed from this planetary encounter. In practical scenarios the incoming and outgoing paths of the object are not parallel, hence the boost obtained is less than in our hypothetical example, but still significant.

Real life applications of the technique are the probes we sent out to various destinations in the past. Sending probes toward the inner planets, located between Earth and the Sun, is somewhat easier since the craft travels toward the Sun and accelerates due to the Sun's gravitational pull. On the converse, sending space craft toward the outer planets is more difficult because the craft must move against the gravity of the Sun, hence in this case the gravitational sling is useful.

The very first use of this technique was demonstrated by the Mariner 10 aircraft launched in 1974. The aircraft used the gravitational field of Venus to accelerate. It is now about 10 billion miles from our Sun. It is in the outskirts of our solar system and is in transition to interstellar space.

Figure 6.2 shows the specific use of the sling shot technique by the Cassini spacecraft launched in 1997. The craft was launched toward the inner planets and used the gravitational field of Venus twice to accelerate. Between the two Venus swingbys the craft completed an elliptical orbit around the Sun, resulting in another Earth encounter a couple of years after its launch. This was then followed by performing another slingshot maneuver around Jupiter in 2000, and in 2004 the craft arrived at Saturn.

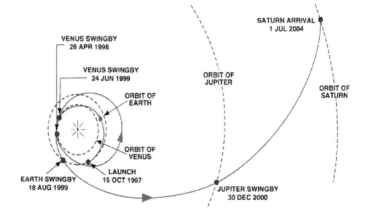

FIGURE 6.2 Cassini sling

Now that we have recognized and utilized the force of gravity, we can think about the absolute escape of it by achieving weightlessness. Weightlessness is not the lack of gravity, it is the lack of the effect of gravity causing our weight. That occurs during free fall. Clearly gravity is still acting on us by accelerating our body, but we do not feel its effect (our weight) as a reaction force on the ground.

An artificial weightless environment may be created in airplanes entering into a steep dive. It is usually a several miles long parabolic arc during which, in the descending phase, the occupants feel weightless. In free fall the acceleration of gravity acts in the same direction as the falling person's velocity, constantly increasing it. That is until the airplane turns the bottom of the dive, at which point the occupants have to endure a double effect of gravity acceleration. Most of these aircraft are used to train astronauts, however, there are now opportunities for brave and rich tourists to fly on private enterprise managed weightlessness flights.

The application of Newton's law of gravity to the solar system enables us to compute the masses of our celestial objects based on their visually measured orbits. In space with no air resistance a planet will retain its orbit due to the force of gravity acting on it. In fact the law describing the orbit of a planet around the Sun, Kepler's first law, may be derived mathematically from Newton's law of gravitation, but it exceeds the intended level of mathematics in this book.

In the case of a single planet and the Sun, the orbit derived is an ellipse. The period of the orbit depends on the size of the orbit. However, in our solar system there are more planets. The influence of the planets on each other, besides their Sun controlled motion resulted in some aberrations from the single planet orbits leading to the discovery of some of the yet invisible objects of our rotational world.

Such unexplainable motion of Uranus, for example, was attributed to the presence of another celestial body outside of its orbit. Newton's theory of gravity was able to predict the existence of a planet not known yet. The later discovered planet was Neptune.

Another planet's unfitting orbit, however, led to the de-throning of Newton's theory. There was another anomaly noticed in the orbit of Mercury in the second half of the 19th century, that was not accountable by Newton's laws. A search for another planet, orbiting even closer to the Sun and invisible to us, was afoot to the extent of even naming it a priori Vulcan. The search was, however, fruitless. Vulcan became the planet that never was.

The discrepancy was ultimately explained by Albert Einstein, likely the most famous scientist in history. Einstein was born in Ulm in Southern Germany in 1879 and had his elementary and middle school education in Munich. He moved to Switzerland in 1896 and enrolled at the university. He was a lackadaisical student, content with studying only topics that captured his interest. Fortunately for humankind, that included physics. His less than spectacular academic record did not get him a university position upon graduation in 1900, resulting in his employment at the Swiss patent office.

Apparently the job provided an environment conducive to pursue his interest in physics and contemplate his, now famous, mental experiments. Those lead to his most important notion that motion is never absolute, it is relative to the frame of reference of the observer. He attributed this to a childhood recognition of the direction of rain-drops when observed from a train. He noticed that when the train was at a station, the rain was falling vertically. When the train pulled out of the station, the rain-drops appeared to fall in a slant direction.

He continued this observation with various mental experiments, such as imagining a person sitting on the train station observing some event happening on a moving train. The different perception of those events by the two observers (one stationary and one moving) led him to his seminal work on the special theory of relativity published in 1905. The work brought him the coveted academic positions, Nobel prize and a worldwide adoration of "the scientist who discovered the truth about our physical world", as said the headlines of the times.

Einstein's description of the space being deformed by large masses made several unexplained celestial phenomena sensical. His interpretation of the gravity is based on imagining the space (for the moment in two dimensions) as a large flexible sheet, like the one the fire fighters (at least in movies) hold stretched out for falling bodies. If we imagine a large ball in the center of the sheet, we can envision that it is going to deform it. The curvature of the deformation of the sheet will be larger the closer we get to the ball producing it.

Placing a smaller ball somewhere on the sheet, it will obviously roll toward the large ball, due to this curvature and manifesting the effect of gravity. Let us assume now that the smaller ball is released by rolling it on the sheet in a circular direction. The ball will still gradually reach the center ball on the bottom of the sheet, however, it will take a few circular orbits around the center. The closer the ball is getting to the

center ball the more aggressive radial acceleration it
will accrue.

Einstein conjectured that the behavior of Venus is
not exactly according to Newton's law of gravity because very close to the Sun those equations are not
accurate. He presented his theory of general relativity in 1915 that accounted for the accurate behavior.
Even more interestingly, Einstein's theory explained a
lot of phenomena related to the behavior of light and
that aspect of it is the most important, but beyond
our mechanical focus here.

Incidentally, as Newton's theory turned out to be in-
complete, so did Einstein's. He spent the decades after
the success of the 1910s trying to reconcile his theory's
shortcoming with the physics of the very small, the
quantum world. He did not succeed and the physics
of subatomic particles is still a challenging scientific
frontier of humankind.

In any case, Newton's theory of gravity is sufficient
to explain most everyday physical phenomena on our
Earthly scale, hence it remains in everyday use. A
spectacular demonstration of the fact that gravity is a
mutual force is related to our oceans. The very familiar
system of tides is a clear indication of the Moon's gravitational pull. However, there still remained some aspects of the Earth's own motion that defied the purely
gravity based explanation.

7

Spinning Earth

The spinning of Earth around its own axis was hypothesized by ancient astronomers for millenea. Proving it was, however, not an easy feat. The biggest problem was that one could not feel the rotation of Earth and it is not a surprise; we cannot feel it today either. How can one prove the rotation of Earth? It was a question that baffled scientists for centuries until finally in 1851 the French Foucault succeeded in answering it.

Léon Foucault was born in Paris in 1819 and was another scientist who started studying medicine and turned to physics later. In his case it was mainly due to his late recognized fear of blood, certainly a hindrance when one wants to pursue the medical profession. His first physics interest was the speed of light and he attempted to measure it. His result was surprisingly good at 298,000 kilometers per second, considering the time and the equipment available to him.

His experiment in 1851, demonstrating the rotation of Earth around its own axis, brought him instant fame and plenty of accolades. He received the medal of the Royal Society and was named the Physicist of the Royal Observatory in Paris. Foucault used the dome of the Pantheon building in Paris to suspend a 28 kg weight with a 67 meter long wire. The long pendulum was released from one side of the building and, as was known from prior experiments, it was expected to hold its plane of swinging. The pendulum, however, apparently continuously changed its plane, demonstrated by its tip drawing a pattern in a sand pit, as shown on Figure 7.1.

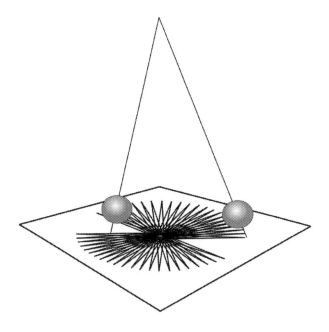

FIGURE 7.1 Foucault's pendulum

The plane of the pendulum's swing rotated clockwise about 11 degrees per hour, hence it was highly visible with a small duration of observation. The pendulum completed a full circle in about 32 hours. Since the experiment is conceptually simple, it provides the basis of many modern day Foucault pendulums at observatories world-wide. Two prominent examples are the one at the Smithsonian Museum in Washington and another one at the Griffith Observatory in Los Angeles. Most modern versions knock over dominoes standing on the perimeter of a circle underneath a dome. Having a domino at every 5 degrees, the pendulum will knock one over roughly in every half an hour to the delight of the visiting audience.

The actual duration of the experiment depends on the latitude of the location where it is executed. At the North Pole, for example, the complete circle would take exactly 24 hours. Conversely, a pendulum suspended on the equator would not show the phenomenon at all. In both cases the plane of the pendulum swing is retained of course, but Earth's rotation produces the different outcome.

At other latitudes the pendulum's swing is somewhere between the polar and equatorial behaviors, and the time of completing the circle varies. The change in the angle of the plane of the pendulum at a latitude angle of φ is proportional to $sin(\varphi)$. Specifically, the change in the rotation angle of the plane is $360 \cdot sin(\varphi)$ degrees per day.

At the pole the latitude angle is 90 degrees, where the sin function is one. Hence the full rotation of 360 degrees takes a day. At the equator the $sin(\varphi)$ is zero and there is no change of the plane of the swing. At an intermediate latitude the $sin(\varphi)$ is less than one, resulting in less than 360 degree rotation a day. Consequently, more than 24 hours are needed to complete the circle, like the 32 hours at the Paris latitude.

Having proven the rotation of the Earth around its own axis brings us to the question: How does Earth maintain its rotation after millions of years? Why are the orbital rotations of Earth around the Sun or the Sun along with our planets around the center of our galaxy still continuing and not seeming to slow down?

Well, the answer lies in this magical quantity called angular momentum and the principle of its conservation. The angular momentum of a particle with mass m and rotating with a circular velocity v at a distance r from the axis of rotation is $m \cdot r \cdot v$. The circular velocity of the spinning particle is well known from high school physics as $v = r \cdot \omega$, where ω is the angular velocity. With this the angular momentum of the particle becomes

$$m \cdot r^2 \cdot \omega.$$

The conservation principle is demonstrated in everyday circumstances by the spinning body of an ice skater. When extending the arms away from the body the rate of the spin slows down and when the arms are pulled close to the body the spinning accelerates. This is because the angular momentum contained in the spinning body remains constant, ignoring the small friction arising in the connection with the ice. Extended arms mean larger radius of the body and conversely, pulled in arms a smaller radius. Since the mass of the skater does not change, the angular velocity must, accordingly.

For the Earth we need to take into consideration all particles and their locations. This requires a bit more algebra as there are a considerable number of particles in Earth and their location is not always on the surface. Hence, the integration of the above formula throughout the volume of the Earth results in approximately

$$M \cdot R^2 \cdot \omega,$$

where we ignored the constant of the integration. M is the total mass of the Earth and R is its mean radius. If we use Earth's radius as approximately 6 million meters, the middle term in our equation becomes roughly $36 \cdot 10^{12}$ or thirty six trillion.

We can compute Earth's angular velocity from the fact that it takes 24 hours to make a full revolution of 360 degrees, or 2π radians, hence it is about $\omega = 2\pi/(24 \cdot 3600) = 0.000073$ radians per second. A radian is the angle one obtains in a circle when the radius is measured up on the circumference. It is approximately 57.3 degrees. Multiplying, the order of the last two terms is still in the billions. If we consider the mass of the Earth also, we are facing an unfathomable amount of angular momentum, at least in our meager human units.

On the next level, Earth has an even bigger angular momentum with respect to its motion around the Sun. The radius of rotation is then the orbit of the Earth around the Sun, about 150 million kilometers, or 150 billion meters. This amounts to $R^2 = 2.25 \cdot 10^{22}$. Even though the angular velocity will be much smaller because now one year is required to make a full circle, hence $\omega = 2\pi/(365 \cdot 24 \cdot 3600) = 0.0000001$ radians per second, the order of the last two terms is still around 10^{15}, or a thousand trillion. Multiplying that again by the mass of the Earth and now we are contemplating a truly out of this world angular momentum.

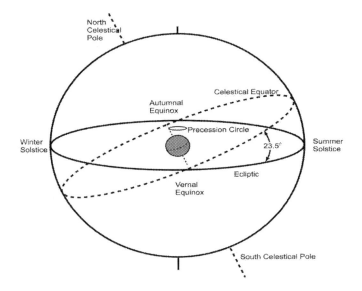

FIGURE 7.2 The precession

Conservation of this angular momentum in space, lacking any conventional friction, is simple. The angular momentum of the Earth moving around the Sun is balanced by the gravitational pull of the Sun, and to a lesser extent the Moon and other celestial objects. The result is the precession phenomenon, the wobbling of the Earth's axis shown on Figure 7.2. It is due to the fact that the combined gravitational pull on Earth is at an angle with Earth's orbital plane, tilting it at an angle of 23.5 degrees.

The tilted position, contributing to the seasons on Earth, was already noticed in the antiquities. Egyptian and Babylonian records a couple of thousand years apart reported different locations of the vernal (spring) equinox in the sky. Vernal equinox is the point on the celestial equator where the path of the Sun crosses it from north to south. The celestial equator is the projection of Earth's equatorial plane to the celestial sphere.

The crossing occurs on March 21st, that is the day when Sun is directly overhead at the Equator and the day and the night are of equal length. The Babylonian records indicated the location of the vernal equinox to be in the Aries constellation while the Egyptians noted it as being in the Lyra constellation. Hipparchus, in 100 BC noticed this discrepancy.

Hipparchus lived on the island of Rhodes, another Greek scientist of those times whose life is less known but whose contributions survived the millenea. He computed the length of the precession cycle by observing the fixed stars. His computations resulted in a rotation of about one degree per century, amounting to a full cycle of approximately 36,000 years. While his interpretation of the observations was correct, he was unable to explain them without the gravity concept that came almost two thousand years after his time.

It is stated in various sources that the phenomenon was at least observed, albeit not understood, by others a long time before Hipparchus, notably the ancient Indians, the Egyptians and the Mayans. According to certain interpretations of ancient Hindi texts, the full revolution was believed to be about 25,000 years translating their units.

More interestingly, some scholars posit that at the time of the building of the three great pyramids on the Giza Plateau the vernal equinox was pointing to the Orion group. The arrangement of the three pyramids is apparently in agreement with the positioning of the three stars creating the Orion figure's belt. Considering the long, several thousand years of history of the Egyptian culture, it is very probable that their celestial observation records were carried over the generations and the changing equinox may have been noted.

The most controversial is the Mayan's knowledge about precession. It is now said by some scholars that the apparent end of the Mayan calendar in 2012 is related to the fact that a full precession cycle is about to be completed in that year. But the beauty of the rotational motion, and the reason it is the worthy topic of this book, lies in its contiguous repeatability. So what could be so specific about the precession position in 2012?

It is predicted that the precession will result in a position during the year 2012 that aligns the Sun with the center of the Milky Way. Adding to this that in 2012 the Sun will be eclipsed twice, by Moon on June 4th followed by Venus on June 6th, and suddenly people see ominous things about that year with double eclipses. We are not going down that avenue and assume that this might just have been a good point to designate as the starting and repeated ending point of the 26,000 year cycle. The Mayans probably did not mean to convey any apocalyptic vision by ending their calendar there; it may have been their superior understanding that the cycle will just end there and start again.

The full precession, we now know more accurately, takes about 25,771 years during which the Earth completes a full wobble. It takes about seventy-two years for the precession angle to change one degree, hence Hipparchus was off by about 30 years. We now fully understand the precession phenomenon and also the reason for the Earth's reluctance to give up its axis of rotation. Remember the childhood spinning toys, the wizzers with the pull string or the simple tops that delighted kids for about a hundred years all over the world? It was magical when we tried to tip it over and it stabilized itself after some wobble and kept on spinning. Well, the same magic is at work with the Earth, called the gyroscopic effect. We are all living on a huge celestial gyroscope.

The gyroscope effect has been known for about 200 years and was demonstrated with various mechanical components, spheres, disks and cylinders. Such objects when spun around their axis of symmetry at a high speed, tend to maintain their state of spinning when mildly disturbed. This effect is also due to the angular momentum. The larger the angular momentum (the faster the object is spinning) the larger the inertia of the object is against changing its orientation. Hence a gyroscope is maintaining its orientation despite the external force's attempt to topple it over.

The hero of our chapter, Foucault himself is credited with giving the name to the instrument. Further inspection of the behavior of the gyroscope reveals other intriguing forces resulting from the rotational phenomenon.

8

Centrifugal feeling

We all have experienced the feeling on the merry-go-round of being pushed toward the outside, or being pushed against the door of a car when turning at high speed. The amusement parks with their legions of high speed topsy-turvy rides make us believe that there is a strong force in action. The force, called the centrifugal force, is probably the most frequently felt in everyday circumstances.

What creates that force and how big is it? Not surprisingly, the force is the outcome of the rotational motion of our bodies around a center point. The strength of the force is related to our distance from the center (r) and the angular velocity ω. Certainly our mass (m) contributes as well, resulting in a simple formula of the magnitude of the force as

$$mr\omega^2.$$

The centrifugal force, shown in Figure 8.1, appears to emanate outwards from the center of rotation and attempts to expel the body in a radial direction if something did not hold it back. That something may be the side of the car or the amusement park ride, and in the planetary scale the counteracting force is the gravity induced weight.

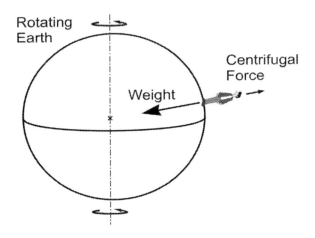

FIGURE 8.1 Centrifugal force

The centrifugal force is only present inside a rotating system. When there is no rotation, there is no centrifugal force. Sitting on an idle merry-go-round certainly will not generate the joy of the ride and the feeling of the outward force. Hence the centrifugal force is not an active force, it is an inertia force.

Inertia forces are always present when a body is accelerating. When we sit on a train that is suddenly accelerating, our bodies drop back against the seat if we face the direction of the acceleration, or we lean forward if we face backward from the train's direction.

When ascending in an express elevator of a high rise building, we are being pushed against the ground with a buckling feeling in our knees. Conversely, the sudden drop of a descending elevator gives us a "lifting off the ground" feeling.

Inertia forces abound, whether we recognize them as such or not. The ultimate thrill of lovers of roller coasters is from the sudden accelerations, decelerations, drops and turns. They are various embodiments of the inertia forces. Their recognition depends on the position of the observer.

When we look at the rotating merry-go-round from outside, being in a stationary position, we will see that some force moves the seats outward. However, only sitting on the merry-go-round makes us feel the effect of that (the centrifugal) force. The difference is that we are now part of the rotating system and our perception has changed.

Newton's third law states that for every action there is a reaction. If a force acts on a body and there is no reaction force, the body will accelerate. The companion force of the centrifugal force is the centripetal force. The name of this force is centripetal because it acts in the direction of the center of rotation.

While people actually feel the centrifugal force and consider it active, the centripetal force is the active force and the centrifugal force is the reactive or inertia force. The phenomenon is shown on Figure 8.2 with a hammer thrower. The centrifugal force is trying to move the hammer away from the person, but the per-

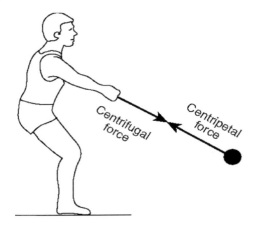

FIGURE 8.2 Centripetal force

son is actually exerting the counteracting centripetal force in the rope.

What happens though, when the rope is released from the hand amidst rotation? The ball will be ejected tangentially from the circle and not radially. This is the consequence of Newton's first law stating that a body retains its constant velocity motion if no external forces act upon it. The rotating ball has a circular velocity due to the rotation and when released it continues along that direction.

This phenomenon is utilized by the hammer thrower to achieve a great distance of the thrown ball. The ability to spin fast thereby achieving a high circular velocity and the timely release are the crucial components. Of course higher circular velocity results in larger centrifugal and centripetal forces in the rope and the thrower's arms, requiring a significant upper body strength.

Another interesting aspect of the centrifugal force is that it seems to have a source in the axis of rotation and spread out therefrom. It is even increasing the farther one (in the rotating system) is away from the center. That is of course simply visible from its equation, the higher the r value is, the larger the force becomes. That is because the larger the radius, the larger the circular velocity gets for a given rotational speed, and when a body is moving straight with a great velocity, a very large force is required to change its direction. Football players trying to tackle a heavy running back moving at high speed know that from experience: it is not that easy to knock them off their path.

Having established in the last chapter that the Earth is rotating, just how big is the centrifugal force arising from the rotation of Earth and our position on it? The equatorial radius of the Earth is about $6,378,000$ meters and we computed the angular velocity of the Earth to be 0.000073 radians per second. Hence the centrifugal force attempting to eject a person of 100 kg mass from the face of the Earth is about $100 \cdot 6,378,000 \cdot 0.000073^2 = 3.39$ kilogram meters per second squared, or Newton.

Catering to the readers with preference to the English units, the numbers would change. Since the mass in pounds would be about 2 times higher than in kilograms and the distance in feet would be almost 3 times bigger than in meters, the numerical value would be about six times larger. However, the actual force exerted on the body would be the same 0.34% or about 1/290th of the weight in either unit.

Consequently, our weight in any place of the Earth is vastly bigger than the centrifugal force attempting to expel us. We are, it appears, quite safely anchored on the Earth and in no imminent danger of being ejected. The number above actually represents the worst case scenario at the equator. This value is much less at higher latitudes due to the appropriately smaller radius of rotation.

Another notable sportive manifestation of the centrifugal force is in car racing. At very high velocities the centrifugal force is extremely large, to the extent of endangering the car to spin out of the curve. In order to compensate for that, race tracks are built banking side ways at the sharper curves. That construction results in part of the centrifugal force pointing into the direction of the wheels, as opposed to the side of the car. The drivers can take the curves with a higher speed as a result of that.

Centrifugal force can explain the bulging shape of the Earth at the equator. The so-called oblateness of our planet is due to the centrifugal effect during the formative years billions of years ago. The whirling material, not yet fully solidified enabled some movement outward in the parts of the planet where the radial distance from the axis of rotation is the largest, e.g. at the equator.

The centrifugal force appears in the orbital motion of planets. Assuming a moon is in a circular motion around its planet, the force of the gravity of the planet is trying to pull the moon into the planet. The centrifugal inertia force counteracts and keeps the moon on the circular path. Note, however, that the centrifugal force is not what gives the planet its circular velocity. Neither is the gravity force. That velocity was acquired when the moon was created by whatever impact scenario was playing out at the time.

In fact, we can use the above equilibrium to compute the distance of our Moon. Let us denote the masses of the Earth and Moon to be M and m, respectively. Newton's law of gravity states the force between them as

$$G\frac{Mm}{R_M^2}$$

where the R_M is the yet unknown distance of the Moon from the center of the Earth. The centrifugal force acting on the body of the Moon is related to its rotation around the Earth and by using the earlier formula it is

$$m \cdot R_M \cdot \omega^2$$

Now we know from observation that the rotational speed of the Moon is about $\omega = 2\pi/28$ radians per day. This is obviously based on the observed value of about 28 days the Moon takes to circle around Earth.

The two forces must be equal since the Moon is in a stable circular orbit around the Earth. From this equality we can compute the radius of the Moon's orbit, and it turns out to be about 60 times the radius of the Earth. Using again the equatorial measure of the Earth's radius of 6,378 kilometers, the distance to the Moon is about 400,000 kilometers, ten times the circumference of the equator.

This method is very generic in celestial computations. If the distance of a celestial object from its gravitational master is not known, however, its orbit time around the planet is measured, then the above calculation enables us to compute their distances. This, in the case of distant objects, is a very powerful tool, indeed.

The centrifugal force has tremendous practical importance. Training pilots include understanding the centrifugal force and its consequences to aircraft flight. The banked race car track appears in the flight terminology as banking. The physical phenomenon is the same, directing some parts of the centrifugal force toward the floor, even though there is no connection between the wheels and the ground during flight. When banking the airplane during a turn, the pilot counteracts part of the centrifugal force with the lift generated by the wings.

Utilizing the centrifugal force results in a way of artificially generating high acceleration of a body. This was the standard training tool for fighter pilots and astronauts in the early days of space travel. A small, one person cabin was suspended at the end of a long spoke and rotated at high speed. The person inside was subjected to an acceleration several times bigger than the acceleration of gravity. The machine even made it into one of the early James Bond movies where the villains tried to kill the hero by over-spinning the machine.

Then there is the weightlessness phenomenon in the space shuttle orbiting outside the Earth's atmosphere. The acceleration of gravity is countered by the centrifugal force attempting to eject the craft from the orbit. The outcome is free floating astronauts, just as shown in the pictures from the various space shuttle missions.

Finally, there are now even amusement park rides cashing in on the phenomenon and creating an artificial weightlessness feeling. The riders are positioned against the wall of a cylindrical chamber rotated with an ever increasing velocity, until the riders are pressed against the wall. After that, the floor is dropped away and the riders are surprised by "being weightless", at least in the vertical direction.

It is highly likely that the centrifugal force was felt and maybe even understood by people in the antiquities. The ancient Roman chariot riders, at least in their motion picture reincarnation, experienced violent roll-overs in tight turns in the Colosseum. But it is hard to pin-point a particular hero of this topic who contributed the most, as we were and will be able to do in other chapters.

Nevertheless, with the addition of the centrifugal and centripetal forces, Newton's second law appeared to remain the universal law of motion in everyday circumstances even on a rotating Earth. That was until some other forces were encountered in rotational systems resulting in rather confounding effects.

9

Carnival twists

Who can forget the exhilaration of walking through the rolling barrel at a carnival or in a modern theme park. Walking straight toward the opening on the other side was a guarantee for falling. Smartly walking against the oncoming rotating wall enabled us to cross. If our footprints were recorded on the inside of the barrel, they would have shown an interesting curved path and not a straight line. What happened with our path was that in a rotating system the shortest path is not necessarily a straight line.

The important discovery of Gaspard Gustave Coriolis in the early 19th century opened up an entirely new understanding of the rotating phenomenon. Coriolis, an applied mathematician, made interesting observations when working as an engineer. He realized that some of the known mechanical laws do not accurately describe certain phenomena when they are viewed in a rotational frame of reference. This was our case in the rotating barrel, where we observed certain motions not necessarily obvious.

Coriolis was born in 1792 in Paris, the same year the monarchy was abolished in France; a topic influencing another great French scientist's life, to be introduced in the penultimate chapter. He graduated from France's premiere school, the Ecole Politechnique, and went to work in the engineering corps for several years. After paying his dues and gaining invaluable insight into some practical problems, he returned to his alma mater to teach applied mechanics.

He published a paper titled *Sur les équations du mouvement relatif des systémes de corps* in the early 1830s. The paper dealt with the equations of relative motion of a system of bodies. It was not about the rotation of Earth or the atmospheric consequences of "his" force; those came later by others. Incidentally Coriolis was investigating the operations of water wheels, the ancient equipment we met in Chapter 1, and the transfer of energy between its various stages.

He proposed a force component for rotating systems that now bears his name although he did not call it that. He considered his force being a component of a global centrifugal force, in addition to the conventional one. Nevertheless, his insight into the phenomenon assured his immortality since the now rather famous force was named after him by others.

We can encounter a manifestation of the Coriolis phenomenon when walking on a carousel of the fairgrounds with horses and other animals fixed to the rotating surface; another joyful memory from our childhood or from parenthood. Let us imagine now that after placing our child on a horse in the central circle, we attempt to reach the gate at the outside rail after the carousel had already started. If we were to walk on a straight radial line painted on the carousel toward the perimeter, we would surely miss the gate because of the rotation of the platform.

In order to reach the gate on the rotating platform our path should be curved like inside the barrel. This phenomenon is easy to comprehend: since the platform is rotating but our intended end point is stationary, we need to adjust for the rotation. You, dear reader, are welcome to physically convince yourself when the fair is in your neighborhood the next time.

FIGURE 9.1 The Coriolis effect

Let us now completely forget about the stationary environment around the carousel and mentally con-

sider us confined to the rotating carousel. Imagine
staying on one side of the carousel and playing catch
with someone located on the other side of the carousel.
When we throw a ball to the other person, it must
move in a straight line as shown on Figure 9.1 between
the two silhouettes. The person we aimed at, however,
moved meanwhile due to the rotation of the platform
and is now in the position of the shaded figure. So
did we. The ball is going to miss the person we aimed
at. From the rotated positions' point of view, the ball
moved away from both persons along a curved path.

This is a harder scenario to comprehend, since the
ball flying in the air is disconnected from the rotating platform. To the observer in the rotating system
the ball would be affected by a force steering it away
from the straight line. That force is the Coriolis force.
The leaning of the path to left or to right depends on
whether the platform is rotating clockwise or counter-
clockwise.

The actual magnitude of the force is related to the
speed of the rotation. After all, when the speed of the
rotation is zero and the carousel is stationary, there is
no such phenomenon. A carousel spinning at a high
angular velocity would create a more pronounced leaning to the side. Hence the magnitude of the Coriolis
force is

$$2m\omega v,$$

where the m is the mass of the moving object and v
is its linear speed. The ω, as in the earlier chapters, is
the angular velocity of the rotation.

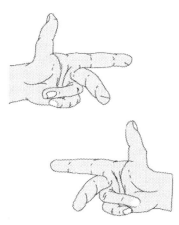

FIGURE 9.2 Left and right hand rules

The direction of the Coriolis force depends on the directions of the rotation and of the motion in the rotating system. It is specified by the so-called left hand and right hand rules shown on Figure 9.2. The left hand rule applies to a counter-clockwise rotation, the right hand rule applies to the clockwise. In both cases we assign the thumb of the hand to the axis of rotation, the index finger to the direction of motion of the object and the middle finger will point to the Coriolis force direction.

Applying these hand rules to our carousel experiment, the curve will lean differently, depending on whether the ball is traveling to north, south, west or east, or on a counter-clockwise or clockwise rotating carousel.

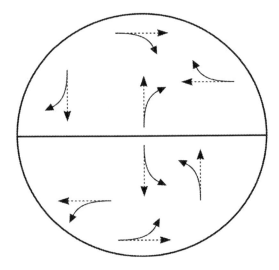

FIGURE 9.3 Coriolis force directions

Figure 9.3 shows various scenarios of throwing a ball on the rotating carousel. The directions applicable to a counter-clockwise rotation are shown on the upper half of the figure. Throwing toward east on a counter-clockwise turning carousel, depicted by the topmost straight arrow on the figure, the Coriolis force will point south. Conversely, throwing to the west the force will be northward. On the other hand, southward throw will result in westward force, while a toss to north will be "deflected" east.

The lower half of the figure represents the directions of the Coriolis force when the carousel is rotating clockwise and they were computed with a right hand rule. Throwing ball on the clockwise rotating carousel toward east, represented by the bottom straight arrow on Figure 9.3, the Coriolis force will point north. All the other scenarios represent an opposite effect of the force between the two rotation orientations.

Since we had a sportive manifestation of the centrifugal force, we'll find one for the Coriolis force also. Many sports involve rotational movement, hence there are interesting examples. An important, albeit not obvious one occurs while playing one of baseball's most difficult positions, shortstop. The problem is catching the ball while facing the home plate, then rotating toward the first base and throwing. In fact, it is akin to our mental exercise on the carousel, except in this case the field is stationary (to a certain extent, we'll ignore the Earth's rotation for this case), but the player is rotating.

Throwing while rotating requires an involuntary adjustment to the Coriolis effect by the player. We can probably just call this talent, as it is unlikely that shortstops in the major leagues ever pay attention to the effect if they know about it at all. It comes with training and experience, but it is there undeniably.

In this baseball example and other real life applications, obviously not all motions (throws in this case) are purely aligned with the geographic directions. The motions of bodies and particles in rotating systems may be generic and the above rules may not be directly followed. The exact mathematical description of such general motions requires the topic of vectors and some of their algebraic operations that are a touch above the intended level of presentation and will be skipped here.

Let it be sufficient to state that the algebraic handling of any general motion will produce consistent directions for the Coriolis force. The directional distinction of the Coriolis force will have great importance when we view its effect on our Earth.

10

Earthly spirals

For simplicity's sake let us assume that Earth is a perfect sphere and ignore the aberrations of the flattening at the poles, the equatorial bulge or the mountains and canyons, no matter how grand they are. On the scale of the Earth and for our topic, they are negligible.

Since Earth spins around an axis that for simplicity is assumed to be connecting the poles, while living on the surface we are permanently participating in a rotating system. We cannot avoid being rotating participants of various physical and meteorological phenomena and our interpretation of some of these is akin to being on the rotating carousel. We will still use the directional components east, north, south and west, however, the axis of rotation of our rotating platform now (the Earth) is not always pointing vertically in the upward direction.

Let us place our location onto the surface of the Earth, somewhere in the northern hemisphere as shown on Figure 10.1. The rotation axis of the Earth at this latitude is not vertical to the observer on that particular local horizon. There is an angle between them that will influence the magnitude of the Coriolis force. Denoting the latitude angle as φ, the magnitude of the Coriolis force becomes

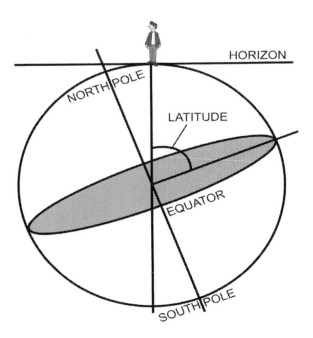

FIGURE 10.1 The latitude

$$2m\omega v \cdot sin(\varphi).$$

When the angle φ is 90 degrees, $sin(\varphi)$ is one, and the Coriolis force is the same as computed in the last chapter. Then we are on the North Pole and the axis of rotation is directed vertically just like in the case of the carousel.

On the other hand when the angle is zero degree, we are on the equator. Then $sin(\varphi)$ is zero and the Coriolis force disappears. This result arose because the axis of rotation of the Earth at the equator is parallel to the horizontal plane. In essence the thumb and the index fingers become collinear at the equator, making the hand rules useless.

The Coriolis effect gets somewhat more involved on the surface of the Earth and has far reaching consequences. Consider the atmosphere. It is controlled by a large number of parameters and it is very difficult to predict the motion of air-masses, i.e. the weather. Sometimes it appears totally random, but actually there is some order in that chaos intriguingly influenced by the Coriolis force.

In the atmosphere, air flows from high pressure areas toward the lower pressure areas, just like heat moves to lower temperatures. Since our atmosphere happens to be on the rotating Earth, it is influenced by the Coriolis force. The straight motion from higher to lower pressure areas will be modified by the Coriolis force to result in the patterns shown on Figure 10.2.

On the figure the longer straight arrows, outside of the circle pointing toward the center, show the intended airflow toward the lower pressure center. The shorter perpendicular arrows indicate the Coriolis force acting sideways. The outcome is the curved arrows of the resulting air movement that will create the counterclockwise revolution around the center. One cannot help, but notice the agreement of this pattern with the carousel experiment and the directional conventions of the last chapter.

Now let's talk about hurricanes. They are in essence nothing else but air moving from higher pressure to

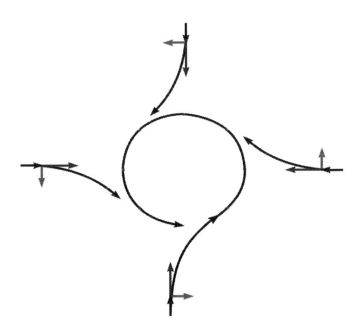

FIGURE 10.2 The Coriolis effect on air movement

lower and they do tend to rotate. The hurricanes of
the Caribbean dominantly rotate counter-clockwise as
expected and the cyclones of the southern hemisphere
clockwise. There appear to be neither cyclones, nor
hurricanes in regions close to the equator, as from the
above equations it is visible that for very low altitude
angles (φ) the Coriolis components are small due to
$sin(\varphi)$ being very small.

By the same token, the value of the $sin(\varphi)$ term
is maximum when the angle is 90 degrees that corresponds to the poles. Overlooking the bit of ambiguity
about which way is east or west when one is stand-

ing on the poles, the horizontal effects of the Coriolis force are at the maximum there. This fact no doubt contributes to the usual rotating weather patterns observed in the polar regions.

FIGURE 10.3 A hurricane

We see distinct spiral patterns on the weather maps of the evening news casts, such as shown on Figure 10.3, depicting a low pressure system photographed by satellites. It is the real life manifestation of the circular pattern seen on Figure 10.2. This is the pattern on the northern hemisphere, the effect of the Corio-

lis force is counter-clockwise. On the contrary, on the
southern hemisphere this motion is the opposite.

There is also an influence of the Coriolis force on
the trade winds, the typical airflow patterns on the
Earth. That phenomenon, besides the high vs. low
pressure air volume movement of the hurricanes, also
involves the temperature. The equator with its hotter
temperatures provides large, rising air volumes. This
hotter air is then turning toward the lower temperature
area at the poles. This northward flow is affected by
the Coriolis force and gets redirected eastward (on the
northern hemisphere), similarly to the hurricanes.

The result is the trade winds, the prevailing air movement between the latitudes from 30 to 60 degrees.
They are called the westerlies since they blow from the
west. Incidentally the trade winds are also westerly on
the southern hemisphere. This apparent contradiction
is due to the fact that the Coriolis effect on a southward motion on the souther hemisphere points to the
west. There are no trade winds at the equator, since
there is no Coriolis effect there. Finally the polar regions, where the Coriolis effect is at maximum, have
notoriously volatile wind patterns.

The high altitude jet-streams are also westerly and
are possibly influenced by the same effects. They are
in the height of 8 to 12 kilometers, or 25,000 to 40,000
feet. Their presence either aids or hinders transoceanic
airline flights, to the extent of about an hour difference
between going with or against the stream. Unfortu-
nately, the air is rather turbulent at the boundaries of
the jet regions, causing trouble to aircraft.

There are other popular beliefs about the effect of the Coriolis force, such as the one about the draining of the sinks in the northern vs. the southern hemisphere being counter-clockwise vs. clockwise, respectively. In reality, scales matter. While there is an undeniable effect at work here, the influence of the actual geometry of the sink is much greater than the Coriolis force. It is easy to see in the modern sinks in our bathrooms today, especially if the faucets are not centrally located, that the water is carried toward the sink hole in patterns influenced by the shape of the sink.

Nevertheless, the effect was proven by some delicate experiments with absolutely symmetrical, cylindrical water tanks with a hole in the center of the bottom. When the water was allowed to become completely still with a long rest after filling, then the plug in the hole was slowly removed, the phenomenon happened. The water drained in the expected directions on both hemispheres.

Then there are some silly superstitions regarding the Coriolis force, like the belief that the common spiral pattern of hair growth on the top of our head indicates northern or southern hemi-sphere origin. This clearly is a myth without any physical foundation, because as we now know, the velocity of the motion also has an influence and the speed of the hair growth in the scale of Earth's rotation is utterly minimal. Another aspect of the scale will also debunk this belief: shouldn't our hair grow straight up due to the much larger centrifugal force than grow in spirals due to the much smaller Coriolis force?

Finally, if possible, the Coriolis force gets even more intricate. The little man of Figure 10.1 moving on a particular latitude plane may ask: How does the Coriolis force recognize the horizontal direction? As we will see, the answer is rather intriguing.

11

Torsional effects

Sometime in the late 19th century a German research group conducted gravity measurements aboard a ship on the North Sea. The resulting data was made available to researchers in Europe and a most intriguing observation was made by scientists. They noted that the measurements were different whether they were made by moving east or west over the same point. This phenomenon was very noticeable and confounded the scientists at the time.

Lóránd Eötvös, scion of a Hungarian noble family, was born in 1848. It was the famous year of his nation's history when Hungary started another ultimately loosing fight for secession from the Austro-Hungarian empire. As usual at the time in Hungarian noble families, Eötvös also entered law school aiming at becoming a politician. His heart was, however, set on natural sciences and after some period he switched to study such at the University of Heidelberg in Germany. He was educated by such luminaries of science as Gustav Kirchoff of the circuit law fame and Hermann Helmholtz, the discoverer of the conservation of energy principle.

After graduation he returned to Pest and obtained a lecturer position at the University of Sciences, now bearing his name (and the alma mater of your humble author as well). His field of expertise was experimental physics and he had a strong interest in gravitation. Eötvös recognized that the direction of Coriolis force depends on the latitude and it is not necessarily in the horizontal plane of the observer. He concluded that the phenomenon encountered by the German scientists was due to the vertical component of the Coriolis force arising at the particular latitude. The effect is since then known as the Eötvös effect and the horizontal plane component of the Coriolis force hence also sometimes called the Coriolis effect.

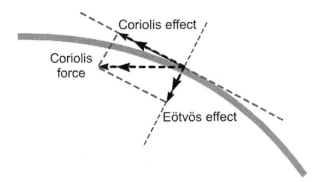

FIGURE 11.1 The Eötvös effect

The vertical component of the Coriolis force at various latitudes is of the form

$$2m\omega v \cdot cos(\varphi).$$

From of our high school mathematics memories we recall that the value of $cos(\varphi)$ is one when the angle is zero. That corresponds to the equator, hence the effect of the vertical component of the Coriolis force is at maximum there. On the converse, there is no Eötvös effect at the pole on account of the value of $cos(\varphi)$ being zero when the angle is 90 degrees.

Combining this with the directional dependence of the Coriolis force one can conclude that moving east the direction of the effect is away from the surface of the Earth. Moving west, the Eötvös effect points into the surface of the Earth, adding to the force of gravity, as visible on Figure 11.1.

The above observations are appropriate for the northern hemisphere, where a counter-clockwise rotation fits the orientation of Earth's rotation vector. This is established by observing the rotation while looking into the axis. On the northern hemisphere, looking south from the pole, the rotation of Earth is counterclockwise. The force would be the opposite in the southern hemisphere, since looking up from the south pole Earth's rotation is clockwise.

Therefore the weight on an eastward moving ship on the northern hemisphere is lessened by the vertical component of the Coriolis force. We are weighing less when we move eastward. Now with some humility we'll have to admit the fact that in the scale of our

personal weight this is unmeasurable, so there will not
be diet plans proposing weight-loss by constantly traveling eastward. Nevertheless, it is another interesting
effect of the rotational phenomenon in our lives.

The actual measurement of the effect is done by a
heavy object suspended on a string. The required sus-
pending force is exactly the same as the gravitational
force, i.e the weight of the object. By the well known
Hooke's law the force in the spring is proportional to
its lengthening. It is rather simple to measure the
length of a spring to a high accuracy, hence the measurement differences between the east and west bound
paths were noticeable.

It is perhaps time to put the Eötvös effect in a quan-
titative perspective. At the latitude angle of 60 degrees, the cosine becomes one half and the vertical
Eötvös effect acting on an object of mass m will simply be

$$2m\omega v\frac{1}{2} = m \cdot 0.000073 \cdot v,$$

where we used the angular velocity of the Earth established earlier in radians per second.

This force, along with the force in the spring coun-
ters the weight of the object. Assuming that a 100
kg object is moving eastward with 10 meters per second, the upward Eötvös force becomes approximately
0.073 Newton. This will lessen the force in the spring,
hence shortening its length. On the contrary, moving
to the west, the vertical force is added to the weight
and therefore further lengthening the spring.

The difference amounts to about a third of an ounce in weight, hence the measured lenght of the spring between the two paths is detectable by a delicate instrument. The effect diminishes as we move toward the poles and increases toward the Equator.

Eötvös' explanation was not immediately accepted. The original German research team, however, repeated the experiment in 1908 on the Black Sea, somewhat closer to the equator. Simultaneous observations were made in two boats independently. The results vindicated Eötvös and his effect was then considered to be fully proven.

Eötvös, the experimental physicist was extremely interested in measuring gravity. He recognized that besides the vertical component of the Coriolis force, the force of gravity acting on a body is also influenced by the centrifugal force and possibly the mass distribution of the Earth. These, he reasoned would be reflected in local changes of the acceleration of gravity that would be a delicate thing to measure, but Eötvös set out to do just that with the help of the mechanical phenomenon called torsion.

An object is undergoing torsion when it is subjected to a twisting around its axis by a torque. For example, a rigid bar held in two hands and twisted in opposite directions by the hands at the ends is experiencing a torsion. Depending on the material of the object, that torsion is most likely invisible. Imagine now twisting a rope at the two ends. The rope is easily and visibly twisted, absorbing the torsion.

The more torque one applies at the ends of the rope, the more resistance the rope will exert. This effect is highly measurable even when small torque differences are applied at the end and was recognized in the late 1700s by Charles de Coulomb. Coulomb measured the electrostatic force between two charged balls with an equipment based on the above principle.

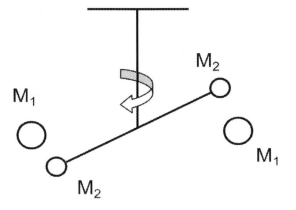

FIGURE 11.2 Coulomb's experiment

In Coulomb's experiment a silk string was the subject of the torsion, clearly an easy to twist material, hence sensitive to very minor force differences. Two pairs of electro-statically charged balls (M_1, M_2) with opposite polarity were brought in close proximity and the pulling force between them was clearly visible in the rotation of the bar. This experiment, shown on Figure 11.2, proved the basis for the law now named after Coulomb.

Some hundred years later, Eötvös decided to utilize Coulomb's equipment in his attempts to measure the local changes in the force of gravity. He realized that the torsion principle afforded a very accurate means to measure minute changes in the direction and strength of the force of gravity. He ingeniously modified Coulomb's equipment by hanging one of the masses with another string from the end of the rod. This arrangement enabled him to detect the local horizontal component of the acceleration of gravity. This became his famous torsion pendulum.

In Eötvös' equipment, revealed in 1891, the string was a platinum-iridium wire with a 0.04 mm diameter; very thin as this is approximately a thousandth of an inch. The horizontal rod was an aluminum tube and the balls had masses of 30 grams or about an ounce. The ball on one side, however, was hanging on another string 65 centimeters (about two feet) below the rod.

The thin string made the arrangement extremely sensitive. At the center point a mirror was attached to the rod reflecting light into a telescope. Even a small change in the rod's orientation was magnified in the changed direction of the reflected light. In case of any discrepancy between the forces acting on the two sides, the rod would rotate and the delicate string mounted mirror equipment would show it.

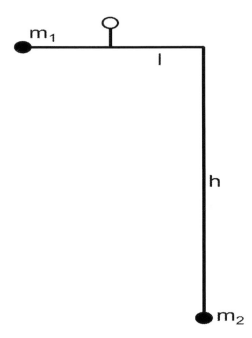

FIGURE 11.3 The Eötvös pendulum

The sketch of Eötvös' pendulum, shown on Figure 11.3, demonstrates Eötvös' thinking. He assumed that if the same horizontal force acted on both balls, the ball hanging on the string would be able to absorb it by slanting the string from its vertical position and producing a moment on the rod. The difference between the horizontal forces on the two ends of the rod would make it rotate.

Eötvös fully understood the fact that the force of gravity is not always vertical. A horizontal force component exist due to the centrifugal force arising from Earth's rotation. This effect is the highest at 45 degree latitude. Incidentally Budapest, the site of Eötvös' first experiments, is at 47.25 degrees latitude, so the site was very well suited for his experiments.

He also suspected that there may be local reasons for additional changes in the horizontal component of the force of gravity. This was not imminently clear, one needed his deep understanding the gravitational phenomenon to accept this. He conjectured that such horizontal changes in the gravity field may be due to masses such as mountain ranges or other tectonic features, as shown on Figure 11.4.

The mass of the Earth on the right hand side of the figure is much denser than on the left hand side. Hence the direction of the gravity force, normally pointing toward the center of the Earth is deflected toward the higher density mass region. This directional change is carried onto the horizontal bar by the string of the lower mass and this will ultimately cause a measurable rotation.

Eötvös was confident that his device would be able to capture this. The sensitivity was spectacular, Eötvös was able to measure a deflection of 1/6000 arc second in the direction of the gravity force, an astonishing number even by today's standards. This was an accu-

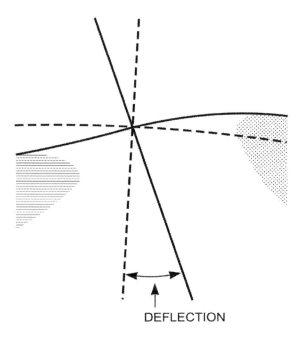

DEFLECTION

FIGURE 11.4 The Eötvös phenomenon

racy far beyond the possible error introduced by the experiment.

Eötvös repeated the experiment with different arrangements, different material components and various orientations. When he calibrated his equipment, in order to minimize the influence of the Earth's local mass distribution under ground, he set the device up on the frozen surface of Lake Balaton in Hungary during a cold winter of 1901. This assured a homogenous mass distribution underneath.

His genial insight into the reasons for the spatial changes of gravity led to his everlasting contribution to science and human life. He concluded that the device should be able to detect sudden changes of gravity force at the boundary of underground deposits of various minerals of different densities than the surrounding region. The rest, how they say, is history.

He proposed in a paper to use his device in searching for oil fields. He in fact demonstrated the use of his equipment in such role by participating in finding the first oil fields in Hungary. By the early 1930s, hundreds of oil fields were found in Europe with the help of Eötvös' equipment.

The equipment was, however, only conceptually simple. The manufacturing required superior craftsmanship and the execution of the experiment needed extreme precision. To avoid the interference of air flow or temperature, the string components of the equipment were enclosed in a metal casing. Special care was applied to the adjustments of the neutral position of the device that employed various adjusting screws.

Due to the delicacy of the equipment, oil producing countries such as the United States, Venezuela, India and Canada purchased their Eötvös pendulums from the original manufacturer in Budapest for decades. Eötvös, the consummate scientist, never patented the equipment despite others' advice. He considered it to be his contribution to humanity. Its conceptual successors are still in use today by geophysicists in oil exploration and mining.

Another seemingly simple rotational phenomenon, the torsional swing of a delicate equipment produced spectacular results. In essence it could be considered a rotary machine of a sort, a predecessor of the many modern machines employing rotational motion to enhance the quality of our lives.

12

Rotary machinery

A very important engineering invention in exploiting rotational motion was the gear. The invention dates back to the antiquities, in fact the hero of our first chapter, Archimedes is credited with inventing a geared odometer to measure the distance traveled by ships. The sketch of Archimedes' device is shown on Figure 12.1.

The external paddle wheel was rotated by the water and its axle inside the ship was equipped with threads engaged in the cogs of a wheel, one of the first occurrences of the concept of a gear. Further consecutive gear pairs gradually reduced the rotation speed to be appropriate for observation on the scale on the top of the box.

Once the gear concept was known, humankind was able to do wonders with the rotational motion. With a properly chosen tooth pairing, the gradation of the rotational speeds became possible. This is the concept utilized even in the bicycle where the rotational motion provided by human pedaling is geared up or down to turn the wheels on the ground slower or faster depending on the terrain. The gear is of course carried much further in our automobiles and other vehicular structures operating under machine power.

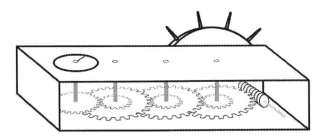

FIGURE 12.1 Archimedes' odometer

Observing repetitive rotational phenomena in the sky was a basis for time keeping since the antiquities. No surprise then, that one of the most widely used rotary machinery became the clock. Combining the gear concept with a little of Newton's gravity results in the weight operated clock. It found employ in the clock towers of medieval cities or in the still popular grand-father clocks.

Their mechanism is simple: a cylinder is rotated by a winding key to roll up a string holding a weight onto the cylinder. The gradual pull of the gravity on the weight will unroll the string from the cylinder and the gear mechanism on the axis of the cylinder will convert that motion into the clock's progression. Two different gears operate the distinct hour and minute arms of the clock at different speeds. Some also have additional time scales, like Moon dials showing the phases of the Moon, requiring a delicate set of gears inside.

Some of the weight operated clocks also contain a chime, a rather loud one in case of the clock towers of towns. This is accomplished by another weight, usually larger than the one keeping the time. Then there are the cuckoo clocks having a birdie pop out once in a while and even sing a melody. Another weight might be used for that purpose. The size of the weight is usually dictated by the torque necessary for the particular operation. The elaborate Glockenspiels in the towers of European towns are driven by very heavy weights suspended on rather long wires to be able to sustain the lengthy dance motion of the characters, a huge tourist attraction in some cities.

Since the gears are built into the clock and hence unmodifiable, the accuracy and the tuning of the clock is accomplished by a pendulum, similar to the one Foucault used. By adjusting the length of the arm, the accuracy of the clock may be corrected. The delicacy of the gear mechanism and the adjustment to achieve a correct time progression are out of our focus, the important fact is that rotational motion enables us to keep time.

The advancement of this technology into the wrist watches added a twist to the mix as the gravity was replaced by winding up a torsional spring. Still rotation ruled, even when the spring was replaced by a battery. We seem to have overcome the need for rotation in measuring time only with the appearance of the digital clocks, but what a ride it was through the centuries. And there are still many, who regularly wind up their wrist watches inherited from their grandfathers.

After being able to keep time, it was time to put the rotational phenomenon truly to work. Perhaps the most important rotary machinery of our lives is the electromagnetic kind. It all started with a Danish physicist, Hans Christian Orsted, who around 1820 demonstrated that a simple magnetic compass is sensitive to an electrical current. The electrical phenomenon itself was in its infancy at the time and Orsted's observation connecting it with the magnetic phenomenon opened up a wonderful world.

Orsted was born in 1777 in Rudkobing in Denmark. His father was a pharmacist and the young Orsted was fascinated with chemistry while growing up. By 1799 he earned his doctorate at the University of Copenhagen and set out to spend several years of postdoctoral studies in Germany where his interest in physics deepened. Upon returning to his alma mater in Copenhagen, he became a professor and spent the following decades in research and teaching.

It appears that his serendipitous discovery of the phenomenon occurred while preparing for an experiment in his lecture with a compass laying on the table. Orsted noticed that when he placed the compass in the proximity of a simple electric circuit powered by a battery turned on, the compass moved. When the battery was turned off the compass regained its natural position, aligned with the Earth's magnetic field and pointed north. It appeared that the electricity flowing through the wire created a magnetic field of its own overriding that of the Earth's.

A few years later, Michael Faraday, an English physicist conjectured that the reverse phenomenon must also exist. Faraday was born about a quarter of a century after Orsted in a London suburb, into a poor family of several children. Hence, after completing his grade school at 14, he was put into a bookbinder apprenticeship to learn a trade. The apprenticeship lasted seven years, during which the young Faraday, eager to learn, read many books on chemistry and physics. By the time he completed his apprenticeship, he had learned enough to be able to follow lectures at the Royal Society using free visitor tickets given away by a charity organization. It was surely an unusual training for a scientist.

Serendipity played a role in his life as well when he obtained the role of an assistant to the known chemist Humphry Davy of the safety lamp fame, one of the distinguished scientists whose lectures he attended. This provided an opportunity for him to access a laboratory where he was able to devise and execute his own experiments.

One of those led to his discovery that a moving magnetic field results in an electric current. His experiment contained a simple closed electric circle without a battery, but with a measuring device. He used a strong permanent magnet and moved it around the wire. Sure enough, the device showed current flowing through the circuit.

He connected that to Orsted's result of a moving electric field producing a magnetic field (moving the compass) and created the since inseparable pair of electro-magnetism. That became the basis of many rotary equipments of our life.

A most important pair, in true correspondence to the principle, is the electric motor and the electric generator. The electric motor produces mechanical energy by a changing electric field, somewhat similarly to Orsted's experiment. Figure 12.3 depicts the concept of a simple electric motor. The wiring surrounds two electric magnets on the perimeter and a permanent magnet in the center constitutes the rotating part. In practical motors there are many more of these components, but the concept is the same.

Systematic change of the electric current in the external (stator) part induces a rotating motion in the internal (rotor) part of the motor. Specifically, the changing current in the stator circuits creates an alternating magnetic field. The field is either pulling the rotor magnet as shown on the upper part of the figure, or pushing as shown on the lower part, depending on the magnetic pole alignments.

The rotor's axle is extended on one side out of the motor enclosure and an application device may be attached to it. There is a wealth of rotary machinery applications in our kitchen, driven by electrical mo-

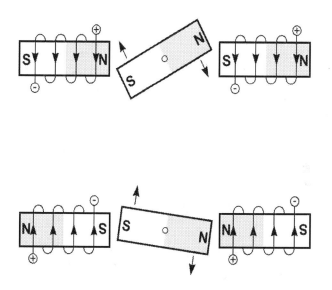

FIGURE 12.2 Electric motor concept

tors. It is noteworthy that their mechanical modus operandi also relies on rotation. All blenders, grinders and mixers do blend, grind and mix their respective subject of operation with rotating motion.

The same principle applies to the hand tools in our life. The widely used hand drills (including the rather dreaded tool of dentists) and the circular saw both attest to the unique applicability of the rotary motion to remove material from a block. Even for tools where a linear motion is needed, like in the case of a surface sanding tool, the power is provided by an electric motor and transfer of the rotating motion is done via a gear.

Industrial machine shops bring another class of rotary equipment. The lathe and the milling machines are nowadays elaborate, computer controlled complexes of multiple, adjustable axes of rotation. The result is automated machining of very delicate shapes with high precision and very brief times. Rotary machinery dominate our manufacturing world.

Centrifugal force is also utilized in various rotary machines. The simple household washing machine's speedy cycle employs the centrifugal force to push the water out of the clothes being washed. In more advanced centrifuges scientists are separating components of mixed materials of different densities, hence inertia. Then there are centrifuges used for nuclear material purification that may again become a main staple of energy supply in the future of humankind.

A reverse manifestation of the electro-magnetic phenomenon, the electric generator, turns mechanical energy provided by some external source into electrical current. The external source could be from any natural resource, such as the wind or moving water.

Wind mills, known for centuries, use a set of simple blades attached to a shaft that is freely rotating under the pressure of the wind. Its childhood toy version, the paper stripes on a small stick we all ran around with, is the proof of the concept working well. In its use in the middle ages, preceding the concept of electricity, the rotational energy obtained on the shaft from the wind was translated into other mechanical uses, such as pulverizing grains or lifting water with a water wheel.

It is worthy of mention here, that the jet stream we met in a prior chapter is on the horizon of scientists considering efficient ways to exploit wind energy. We do not have the technology to harness it yet, but it is estimated that only a small percentage of the jet stream would be able to supply the whole world's energy needs. In the future we may develop technology to tap into that steady energy source.

In modern wind mills the rotating axle of the wheel is extended into a generator enclosure with wiring on the stationary part. The end of the rotor is now the place for the magnets that induce the electrical current in the wiring. There are wind farms in many areas of the world, ranging from the California desert regions to the Scandinavian sea shores.

The concept of scooping up water with a water wheel brings us to the other natural energy source: moving water. In a reverse application of the ancient tool, the water wheel may also be simply subjected to the force of the water allowing the wheel to freely rotate along with the axle it is mounted on. The other end of the axle was driving grain grinding stones already in the middle ages, a device transcending all the early human societies with agricultural culture.

In the modern arrangements, water is gathered up beyond a dam and the water wheels' successors, the water turbines are built into tunnels. The force of the water in the tunnels rotate the turbine blades mounted on rotating axles. On the generator side of the turbine the electricity is produced by a reverse use of the electric motor phenomenon explained above.

Both of these devices, wind mills and water turbines, use abundantly available natural mechanical energy to generate expensive electrical energy. Humankind has an ever increasing energy requirement for the world and needs clean ways of generating it. Hence the rotational energy, obtained by harnessing the power in the motion of the water and air, is still the most promising energy source for the future.

Another extremely important effect of the rotational phenomenon to humanity is of course transportation. We are far away from the time of the introduction of the wheel, but a certain successor of it has an even more profound influence on our lives.

13

Whirling propellers

We observed rotating objects with mainly circular symmetricity so far, but that is far from being a necessity. Propellers, the most important tools of mobility of mankind after the invention of the wheel, are not circular in themselves in stationary position. They have specially shaped blades, and several of them are attached to a cylindrical hub. They are arranged at even angular distances.

The rotating motion of the propeller blade through some medium, like water or air, will produce a thrust on the hub. The thrust will move whatever is attached to the hub (a boat or an airplane) forward in the particular medium. It is of course Archimedes' genial screw concept at work here again, as the propeller will also have a spiral movement in the medium when moving ahead. The so-called pitch of a propeller is the angle between the chord of the blade and the plane of rotation.

The profile of the blade is somewhat different whether moving (in) air or moving (in) water, but we'll ignore that in our focus on the rotating phenomenon. We will also be slightly biased toward ships, due to our reverence to the historical water wheels and Archimedes' screw (as well as to the background of yours truly).

In most ship propellers the number of blades is three or four. The famed but ill-fated Titanic was propelled by two three and one four bladed propellers. Modern cruise ships and tankers have propulsion systems with multiple axles and multiple blades.

Propellers of course exhibit the same rotational phenomena based forces that we observed in earlier chapters. These forces play important roles considering the fact that the rotational speeds of propellers may be very high. Their outcome may be an unsymmetric thrust, with respect to the direction of the forward movement, or the axle of rotation.

A floating ship is free to move in absorbing the undesirable component of the trust, resulting in a various motions. For example, the lateral motion of the yaw is the result of the flow detaching from the propeller and proceeding in the direction of the horizontal arrow on Figure 13.1. To avoid this, most modern ships employ twin propellers that are rotating in the opposite direction, thereby canceling out the undesirable effect.

Incidentally the three major undesirable motions of ships could all be described as certain rotations. Aforementioned yaw motion amounts to a rotation of the ship's body around a vertical axis. The so-called rolling motion of a ship, the side-to-side leaning and the leading cause of sea sickness, is a rotation around the longitudinal axis of the ship. Finally, the pitching motion of the ship, resulting from climbing the wave crests and dipping into the valleys, may be visualized as a rotation about an axis perpendicular to the longitudinal axis of the ship.

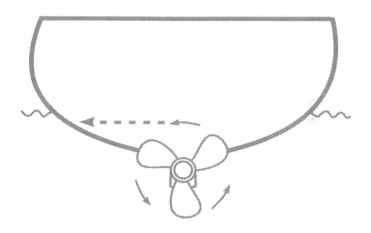

FIGURE 13.1 Ship propulsion

It is also interesting to note that ship propulsions of actual Archimedes screw types were also built without the external cylindrical wall. These were popular and competed with the paddle-wheels during the middle of the 19th century. They were later abandoned and replaced by the propeller types. Ironically, they have reemerged, in fact in an even closer reminiscence to Archimedes' original screw, in the modern water jet propulsions of pleasure boats. It appears that engineering history repeats itself in cycles as well.

The rotational speed of propellers is of utmost concern. When a propeller is rotating at a too high speed, then the water pressure around the blade could drop so low that the water at the given temperature vaporizes. When the vapor bubbles collapse, pressure waves emerge in the water resulting in a pitting force on the surface of the blade, the dreaded cavitation phenomenon. The damage on the blades is serious and the efficiency of the propeller under such conditions is diminished.

Considering the propeller's sensitivity to the rotation speed, there is another aspect of propellers that is noteworthy. That is the fact that they start from a stationary, non rotating position and gradually accelerate their rotational speeds to that of an operational or optimal speed. During this process the angular velocity, that we have so far considered to be constant, changes its magnitude. This was recognized by Leonhard Euler, another giant of the 18th century.

Euler was born in Basel, Switzerland in 1707 and was a child prodigy accepted at the University of Basel at the young age of 13. By his 16th birthday he obtained a Bachelor's degree and in another three years he received his doctorate as well. He accepted a position in the St. Petersburg Academy's mathematics department and spent most of his academic life in Russia apart from a decade in Germany in the middle part of his career.

His mathematical contributions are spectacular, ranging from his number e to his famous formula combining that with another fundamental number, the π. He is considered to be the founder of modern graph theory and various applied mathematics inventions are also in his legacy. The latter interest led him to physics and mechanics, where he provided the first solution to the buckling phenomenon of axially loaded beams, called Euler beams ever since. His recognition that the change of the angular velocity, i.e. the angular acceleration, will result in another force completed the picture of the rotational phenomenon.

The force now named after him as the Euler force has a magnitude of

$$m\dot{\omega}r,$$

where $\dot{\omega}$ is the angular acceleration and r is the distance of the object with mass m from the axis of rotation.

The Euler force is also an inertia force expressing a rotating object's resistance against the acceleration or deceleration of the rotation. It is best understood by considering the simple experiment of spinning a ball attached to a string, as shown on Figure 13.2.

When the spinning begins, due to the Euler force, the ball somewhat lags behind the rotating motion of the hand. After a while an equilibrium is established when the hand and the ball have the same angular velocity. They move in synchrony and during one completed circle by the hand, the ball also completes a full circle. Their respective circular velocities, $v = r \cdot \omega$, are of course different. Even though the angular velocity is the same, the ball is rotating on a circle with

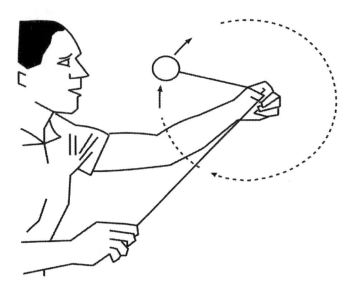

FIGURE 13.2 The Euler force

a larger radius than the hand.

Let us now imagine the hand gradually slowing down its rotation, i.e. decelerating. The ball, due again to Euler's force, will continue to rotate with the same velocity and gets ahead of the hand's rotation. This will ultimately result in an unstable scenario and by the time the hand stops, the ball likely would have fallen out of its circular orbit.

If possible, the direction and the orientation of the Euler force are even more intricate than those of the Coriolis force. The force acts in the plane of rotation, however, its direction is constantly changing following the rotation. Hence it is sometimes called the azimuthal force. The azimuth angle is a specific reference angle used in rotating systems.

Ancient mariners have used this angle to judge their position on the high seas. The angle is obtained by projecting a star's location to the horizon and measuring the angle between that direction and north (identified by the north star or a magnetic compass later). Monitoring the location of a certain star was a simple tool of navigation for millenea. It is now largely replaced by GPS (global positioning system) based navigational tools on the seas and even on land.

As the azimuthal angle changes for the mariner traveling on the rotating Earth, so does the direction of the Euler force acting on an object in a rotating system. The orientation of the Euler force, on the other hand, is dependent on the sign of the change of the angular velocity. When the rotation is accelerating it points forward, into the direction of the circular motion. In the case of a decelerating rotation Euler force points backward, opposite from the circular motion, just like in the spinning string experiment.

This phenomenon contributes to the potential instability of heavy (remember the mass in the force) rotary machinery. The imbalance during the speed-up or the shut-down process results in the so-called backward and forward whirl motions. The first one is when the rotating part is lagging behind the angular speed of the axis and the the latter one is the opposite, both due to rotational inertia.

The azimuth angle remains important in astronomy. Without considering the azimuth angle, the locations of the permanent stars could not be reconciled when viewing them from different places on the rotating Earth, or the rotating solar system. With that, let us look back into the sky to follow our rotational pursuit.

14

Galactic rotations

In the preceding chapters we demonstrated a multitude of roles the rotational phenomenon plays in our lives on Earth. It is now time to see whether those roles extend to the galactic scale.

It is rather peculiar that the planets of our solar system orbit in a common plane. Why is that? The question confounded Newton when he realized the fact that gravity makes the planets move around the Sun. His explanation, based on the prevailing creationary wisdom, was that God must have placed the planets into a plane.

It took the genial effort of Pierre Simon Laplace in France to provide a scientific explanation. Laplace was born about a hundred years after Newton in a small Normandy town into a non-noble family. While serving in the army in 1784, he briefly tutored a young 16 year old cadet from Corsica by the name of Napoleon Bonaparte. Despite Laplace having an apolitical personality at the time, his life was endangered during the tumultuous French revolution at the end of the 18th century. He and his family narrowly escaped the revolting Paris mobs and sought refuge in the countryside.

His time in this self-imposed exile resulted in a monumental five volume work titled *Mécanique céleste*, translated as Celestial Mechanics. In the book published in 1799, literally in the last days of the most tumultuous century of France's history, Laplace was finally able to explain why all celestial objects revolve in the same direction and largely in the Sun's equatorial plane. He described a whirling solar atmosphere as the origin of the arrangement.

Laplace hypothesized that the effect of rotation to a cloud of gas with solid particles resulted in the observed system. If the rotational speed and the density are high enough, the particles of the cloud will gravitationally attract each other and coalesce into bigger chunks. As this process continues, the cloud will rotate faster and faster, somewhat similarly to the ice skater's spinning being accelerated by the skater closing the arms around the body.

The originally spherical cloud will become more and more flattened and the largest chunks of the cloud (the future planets) will orbit in the disk. Since the originally irregularly shaped parts will have inertia forces acting on them, they will start to rotate themselves. That rotation will further shape those chunks into spheres and planets will be formed, as shown on Figure 14.1.

This hypothesis is now commonly accepted. When astronomers looked at young stars, they found that many of them have a surrounding disk of gas and particles. Obviously, we cannot really monitor one of them becoming a system of planets, the celestial time scales are measured in millions of years, but it appears that

FIGURE 14.1 The birth of planets

the process is valid.

The 19th century brought Napoleon back into power, albeit for a short time culminating in his final defeat at Waterloo. During this time Laplace dedicated a volume of his work on celestial mechanics to Napoleon. As the story goes, after briefly leafing through the book Napoleon complained about seeing no mention of God in it, perhaps the first such comment of the historical discourse surrounding the topic. In his later years Laplace became a strong supporter of the Bourbon royal family and Charles X granted him nobility and the Marquis de Laplace title in 1827.

On a side note, it is worth mentioning that Laplace has already written about forces in vortex equations of hydrodynamics in the late 1700s. This may be considered a precursor of his yet unborn countryman, Coriolis' now famous description of the forces at work in rotating systems.

Since the process proposed by Laplace appears to be operational in millions of places in the universe, it is likely that many other solar systems of our kind may have been formed during the billenea of our past. The inevitable conclusion is that extraterrestrial intelligence may also have developed. Some of those may even have visited us before, but this topic is far beyond our rotational focus.

We have just established that rotation played an instrumental role in the forming of our solar system. Let us now move on to the host of our solar system, the Milky Way galaxy and see the instrumental role of rotation on that scale. Milky Way is also rather flat, disk-like and has an assortment of interesting spiral arms. This shape implies that there is some rotation involved there as well.

The Milky Way galaxy is home to another 100 billions suns and solar systems, like ours. The two closest solar systems in our galactic neighborhood are Sirius and Alpha-Centauri. Our galaxy is roughly 140,000 light years in diameter and its thickest part in the center, the bulge, is about 20,000 light years in diameter. The galaxy also contains billions of meteoroids and asteroids, along with hundreds of star clusters.

In the beginning of the last century modern methods of radio wave and X-ray observations arrived in astronomy, certainly more powerful than Galileo's handmade telescope some 300 years earlier. Jan Oort was born in the Friesland area of the Netherlands and studied at the famous Groningen University. His main area of interest was astronomy, especially distant stars and he pioneered the detection of radio waves arriving from them.

Observing the radio waves from many distant Milky Way objects, in 1925 Oort realized that some stars are lagging behind the Sun in their motion while others are bypassing it. This, he recognized, was similar to the motion of the inner planets vs. the outer planets in our solar system. He considered this to be the direct proof of the rotation of the Milky Way, but it was not accepted immediately.

There is now irrefutable evidence that the Milky Way is rotating. There is an eerie resemblance of the computer generated Milky Way picture on Figure 14.2 to that of the hurricane on Figure 10.3. It is quite likely that our solar system may also be controlled by the forces of rotation we seem to have understood by now, the centrifugal and Coriolis forces, as well as the Eötvös effect and the Euler force.

Further observations of Milky Way also established the presence of three major spiral arms, called the Sagittarius arm, the Orion arm and the Perseus arm, in order of their distance from the center of our galaxy,

FIGURE 14.2 The Milky Way

the last being the farthest out. There are several minor arms and some that seem detached from their original major arm.

So where are we in this rotating galactic system? Oort calculated that the galactic center would be about 30,000 light years away from us. We are on a rotational path around the center of the Milky Way on one of those spiral arms, specifically the partial arm of the Orion arm, called the Orion spur. We are also about 15 light years off of the main plane of the disk.

Consequently we rotate around the center of the galaxy at an approximate speed of 234 kilometers per second. At this speed it takes us about 250 million years to complete a rotation, mere minutes compared to the age of the universe, presently assumed to be about 15 billion years. Our solar system is estimated to be about 4.6 billion years old, hence our Sun may have already done about 18 full circles.

It is hypothesized by some astronomers that our solar system was actually born about ten percent farther out, some 33,000 light years from the center and 200 light years off the main plane of the Milky Way. It appears that we are moving toward the central gravity providing object of the Milky Way (the black hole we conjecture it to be now) and on a spiral rotation pattern like some galactic hurricane under the Coriolis force. The apparent clockwise direction of the spiral arms may even mean that we are on the "southern hemisphere" of the galaxy, using the notation rather figuratively.

There are of course other galaxies, beside ours. The universe is estimated to contain about 100 billion galaxies. Our Milky Way is actually a member of a group of about thirty galaxies, called the Local Group. Our closest neighbors are the Magellan cloud and the Andromeda cloud, the latter is a subject of some intrigue in the following. It is safe to assume that the rotational phenomenon played an instrumental role in their formation as well. This begs the question of the applicability of the rotational principle to the intergalactic space and eventually the universe.

After all, if the Milky Way's shape resembles a hurricane, that is the movement of air in the atmosphere of a rotating Earth, then that shape may also imply that it is moving in a rotating universe.

15

Wheels in the sky

From the days of Ptolemy and Copernicus, the bigger picture of the universe was represented by the so-called fixed stars in the sky. The ancient astronomers attempted to establish our position in the universe in reference to those known constellations. This big wheel in the sky, the age old Zodiac is shown on Figure 15.1. The Zodiac was the basis for a medieval branch of astronomy called astrology. It is nowadays considered a pseudo-science at best, but just like the flat Earth belief, it still has followers.

Astrology was based on affixing certain characteristics to the perceived appearance of twelve major galactic constellations, Sagittarius, Scorpio, Libra, Virgo, Leo, Cancer, Gemini, Taurus, Aries, Pisces, Aquarius and Capricorn. Their alignment was associated with certain periods of the year and people born in those periods supposedly inherited the generic personality characteristics of their sign. The horoscope generation was a custom made application of these astrological principles to a particular person's time of birth.

It was also used to interpret the cycles of our life, from birth through adulthood and to death, and in turn giving birth to other lives with their own cycles. There is even an out-shoot of this, called synchronic-

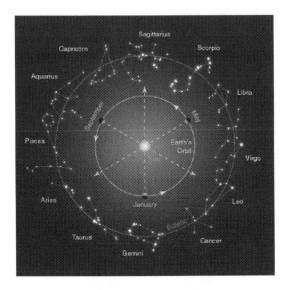

FIGURE 15.1 The Zodiac wheel

ity, that associates certain celestial events with actual Earthly events. This leads into the realm of the speculative, so we will end this train of thought.

Let us return to the astronomical side and reconsider the precession cycle of Earth's axis introduced in an earlier chapter. The 26,000 year precession cycle represents an even bigger wheel in the sky, shown in Figure 15.2. On the figure the number 2000 represents the calendar year 2000, our present celestial north in that big wheel in the sky. The total cycle is shown by going back 10,000 years and going forward about 16,000 years, their sum totaling the precession cycle time.

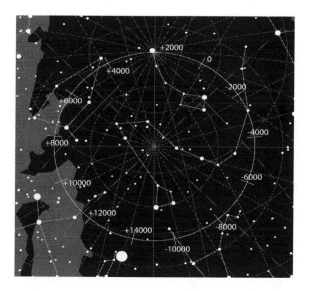

FIGURE 15.2 The precession wheel

The size of the spots in the precession wheel picture indicate the relative luminosity of the stars. The rather bright star to the left of the 2000 year mark is Polaris that is our present North Star. The same concept is applicable to the southern hemisphere. The polar direction of the southern hemisphere, or the South Star is in the Sigma constellation.

The brightest star on the bottom of the picture is Vega in the constellation named Lyra. Vega will become our North Star in about 14,000 years. Polaris will become our North Star again in about 25,700 years or in the year 27,800 AD, assuming that there will not be any change in the current calendar system. We can't be sure whether there will be humans to observe that time period in the life of our planet, but the planet by all celestial indications will still be alighted by the Sun.

Since this wheel in the sky turns too slowly for a human life time, even for human cultures, we do not truly comprehend its effect on our life. The turns of this wheel bring apparent ice ages about ten thousand years apart and some natural warming periods between them, subject of extreme cultural and political upheaval in our society today. We may, however, only have a childish tempest in the universal teapot in that regard.

The next step in humankind's quest was to step outside our galaxy and that was a giant step first taken by Edwin Hubble in 1924. Hubble was born in 1884 on a Missouri farm and as his famous predecessor, Galilei, he also first studied the topic of his father's choice. In Hubble's case this was law, but his private interest was in astronomy. He became one of the first recipients of a Rhodes scholarship and went to Oxford in 1910, where his astronomy interest deepened.

His scientific breakthrough came at the Mount Wilson observatory in Pasadena. After diligent observations for long nights on the cool mountain top, he recognized the fact that the Andromeda Cloud was just too far away to be a part of the Milky Way and it is a galaxy on its own right. This finding destroyed the prevailing single galaxy view of the time. He showed that the universe was full of galaxies and he also conjectured that they are apparently speeding away from each other. The universe is expanding!

This expanding universe does not preclude the possibility of the galaxies rotating, a fact we found very plausible in the last chapter in connection with the Milky Way. Then the physics interpretation in the rotating frame of reference of the universe may also include a certain manifestation of the Earthly phenomena of the centrifugal and Coriolis forces, the Eötvös effect and Euler force, as well as gravity on a truly universal scale.

But the rotating galaxies seem to have an apparent discrepancy between the masses of galaxies conjectured based on their luminosity and the masses required to account for their motion. An explanation, presently accepted by scientists in the know, states that the discrepancy is due to material that has no luminosity hence invisible, the so-called dark matter. As many radically new ideas in astronomy, it is only grudgingly accepted. While it approximately explains the newest observations of certain stars moving within other galaxies, we have no concrete proof for its existence.

The orderly rotating vision in the sky is sometimes disturbed. Intriguingly the Andromeda galaxy, Hubble's subject of observation appears to be on a collision

course with the Milky Way. That is of course in the
realm of possibilities, after all there are loose planetary
objects in our own solar system as well. Since those
defy the general rotational scheme of things, there
could be rogue galaxies in the intergalactical space too.

As in the carousel experiment, then later with the
Earth and the solar system, we always used a reference
system with respect to which the rotating phenomenon
was measured. However, if our universe is infinite as
put forth by many scientists, then there should not be
anything outside of it. Then there would be no external reference system, hence the universe could not be
rotating.

This scenario, of the universe being all encompass-
ing, immobile and infinite, requires an explanation of
the origin of the material in this unique universe, the
creation of the gas-dust clouds in various places of the
universe, and the central masses controlling the rotation of the galaxies. It is presently explained, although
not universally accepted, that the origin is an infinitely
small, infinitely dense primordial material soup preceding an explosion called the big bang. This hypothesis appears to be supported by Hubble's expanding
universe observation, but it still requires a big leap of
faith to believe that, since we do not know physical
laws that would govern the phenomenon.

This issue of the creation of the original material
is not to be confused with the formation of the stars
and planets. Many of those phenomena are now indisputable and many still are hypothetical. The issue
is much deeper and gets as philosophical as physical.

After all, if the universe was finite and there was a hyper-universe around it, our universe could be rotating with respect to an axis specified in that hyper-universe. This would be the biggest wheel in the sky, the mother of all wheels.

There are ongoing attempts trying to quantify the rotation of the universe. It is presently conjectured to be an extremely slow rotation completing a turn in about 60,000 billion years. This so-called "universal vorticity" translates into about 10^{-12} degrees per year angular velocity. The question is, with respect to what? This is a question with profound implications.

We seem to have a very good understanding of the workings of our solar system that may be carried to our galaxy and to the known universe. But when reaching beyond, we require an inquisitive mind not satisfied with the standard explanation of the big bang. The glaring singularity in the beginning of that hypothesis leaves room for other ideas and a potential proof of the rotation of the universe may reveal some hidden facts regarding its creation.

If the axis of rotation of our universe is located in a hyper-universe, then the phenomenal effects of rotation could work on an even higher scale. This scenario opens up the possibility of or our universe having been created in this hyper-universe. Whether it was by a higher power, anthropomorphic or not; a physical-chemical process or an intelligent design, it is immaterial. The important fact is: there is room in the hyper-universe for the creation to unfold.

Some kind of a creation is of course a proven fact by our mere existence. Had it not been for the creation of the original material components, whatever they were and however they happened to come into being, we would not be here today. We can safely say, however, that the rotational phenomenon was, is, and will always be a crucial component of the physical universe.

The wheels in the sky keep on turning!

Epilogue

We saw that the gradual understanding of the rotational phenomenon as it applies to our solar system is one of the greatest epics of human history. It is filled with cultural division and religious opposition, all to be overcome by physical evidence and the strong personae of the scientists involved.

The scale of the rotational phenomenon is also very important, especially when the rotating motion of extraterrestrial objects of our galaxy is observed. The size of a human being is on the order of a meter, most people are in the range of 1.5-2.0 meters (between five to six feet) in height. Our cosmic horizon, the distance we can see at the moment (not visually of course), is about 10^{26} meters, something that we cannot put into everyday words in our units. One can say that humans expanded their horizon from the size of their being with about 26 orders of magnitude. Astonishing, almost incomprehensible, but it is true.

What about narrowing the horizon? Looking inside, into our bodies, at the materials we and the world are comprised of, is another interesting journey one can take. That road also goes through various rotational phenomena, starting from the first detailed, so-called planetary model of the atoms. That model posited a nucleus of the atom surrounded by electrons on circular patterns in an eerie resemblance to our solar system.

This was later improved by recognizing that the electrons' orbits are matching certain energy states and when they change orbits, some new particles are ejected. The concept of various rays such as alpha and gamma emerged. Even more interesting is the fact that it was also found that the orbiting electrons, besides the angular momentum of their orbit around the nucleus (like Earth's angular momentum in its orbit around the Sun), also have a spin (again like Earth does around its own axis of rotation). The similarities are even more striking if we consider that this phenomenon is now played out in the scale of about 10^{-16} meters.

Very likely it does not end here, as the continually discovered sub-particles prove. Since the traversing of the 26 orders of magnitude outward took millenea, but the traversing the 16 orders inward happened mainly in the last one hundred years or so, there is obviously much more to learn in that direction. We only have rudimentary understanding of the physics of the sub-atomic scale. Perhaps in another hundred years we'll even out our external-internal playing field in God's playground.

Literature

[1] Anthony, H. D.; Sir Isaac Newton, Abelard-Schuman, London, 1960

[2] Asimov, I.; The universe: from flat Earth to quasar, Walker, New York, 1966

[3] P. Birch; Is the universe rotating?, Nature, pp 451-454, July 29, 1982

[4] Chapman, A.; Gods in the sky, Channel 4 Books, London, 2002

[5] Einstein, A. and Infeld, L.; The evolution of physics: From early concepts to relativity and quanta, Simon&Shuster, New York, 1938

[6] Ellis, W. M.; Ptolemy of Egypt, Routledge, New York, 1994

[7] Ferguson, K.; Tycho and Kepler, Walker, 2002

[8] Garwood, C.; Flat Earth, The history of an infamous idea, St. Martin's Press, New York, 2007

[9] Gillispie, C. C.; Pierre-Simon Laplace, 1749-1827, Princeton University Press, New Jersey, 1997

[10] Gingerich, O.; The great Copernicus chase and other adventures in astronomical history, Cambridge University Press, Cambridge, 1992

[11] Hirshfeld, A. W.; Eureka man: The life and legacy of Archimedes, Kindle, 2009

[12] Hirshfeld, A. W.; The electric life of Michael Faraday, Kindle, 2009

[13] Király, P.; Eötvös and STEP, Proceedings of WPP, ESTEC, Noordwijk, 1996

[14] Livio, M.; The accelerating universe, Wiley, New York, 2000

[15] McCluskey, S. C.; Astronomies and cultures in medieval Europe, Cambridge University Press, 1998

[16] Naess, A. and Anderson, J; Galileo Galilei - When the World was still, Springer, Berlin, 2005

[17] Nicastro, N.; Circumference: Eratosthenes and the ancient quest to measure the Globe, StMartins Press, New York, 2008

[18] Primack, J. R. and Abrams, N. E.; The view from the center of the universe, Penguin, New York, 2006

[19] Sagan, C.: Cosmos, Random House, New Jersey, 1995

[20] Tobin, W.: The life and science of Léon Foucault: The man who proved the Earth rotates, Cambridge University Press, 2003

Index